WRITING
COMMERCIAL
FICTION

WRITING COMMERCIAL FICTION

John Stevenson

Prentice-Hall, Inc., Englewood Cliffs, New Jersey 07632

Library of Congress Cataloging in Publication Data

Stevenson, John (date)
   Writing commercial fiction.

   Includes index.
   1. Fiction—Authorship.   2. Popular literature—
Authorship.   I. Title.
PN3365.S83 1983   808.3   83-3183
ISBN 0-13-971689-0
ISBN 0-13-971671-8   (A Reward book : pbk.)

For Jim and Rosalie

This book is available at a special discount when ordered
in bulk quantities. Contact Prentice-Hall, Inc., General
Publishing Division, Special Sales, Englewood Cliffs, N.J. 07632.

10 9 8 7 6 5 4 3 2 1

ISBN 0-13-971689-0

ISBN 0-13-971671-8 {PBK.}

Editorial/production supervision by Maxine Bartow
Cover design by Hal Siegel
Manufacturing buyer: Pat Mahoney

Prentice-Hall International, Inc., *London*
Prentice-Hall of Australia Pty. Limited, *Sydney*
Prentice-Hall Canada Inc., *Toronto*
Prentice-Hall of India Private Limited, *New Delhi*
Prentice-Hall of Japan, Inc., *Tokyo*
Prentice-Hall of Southeast Asia Pte. Ltd., *Singapore*
Whitehall Books Limited, *Wellington, New Zealand*
Editora Prentice-Hall do Brasil Ltda., *Rio de Janeiro*

Contents

THE PLOT

CHARACTERIZATION

THE ACTUAL WRITING

Foreword

When John Stevenson and I were forty years younger, the best way to break into the writing field was with short stories. But *Collier's* and *Argosy* and the pulps have died away, and with all those hundreds of great old magazines gone, virtually no market remains for short fiction. What's left for the beginner—the budding author not yet ready to write the Great American Novel? The answer is genre fiction—romance, mystery, family saga, western, gothic, science fiction, fantasy, and occult. They are relatively easy to write (far easier than short stories) and, more to the point, easier to sell.

The goal of most of us who presume to call ourselves writers is to one day produce our personal masterpiece. But getting it written takes more than talent and more than luck. It takes experience in plotting, in making characters come alive on the page, in making situations work and scenes seem real. One can get that experience by writing for the desk drawer, but it's a frustrating business and no substitute for seeing one's words printed between covers. If genre fiction is the best and easiest way to get this experience, then how does one go about writing genre fiction?

The best answer I've ever seen to that question is now on my desk. It's the manuscript for John Stevenson's *Writing Commercial Fiction.* Stevenson is a professional's professional—the author of genre books that range across the spectrum from romance-suspense to action-adventure to espionage. Had I seen this manuscript around fifteen years ago when I was laboriously pecking away at my first attempt at suspense, it would have cut my labors in half. John seems to have encountered all those problems, all those dead ends, all those debacles of plotting and characterization that so bedeviled me in my earlier books. I suspect they're the same problems you'll confront—universal hazards. John's analysis of their causes and prevention will be of immense help to a beginner. I find they're helping me now, and I've been writing almost as long as Stevenson.

He starts by defining the various genres and helping you make your selection; he tells how to construct your plots, create your characters, and put them all together. He tells about the most essential part of any book—the first few paragraphs—how to keep it going until the end, and what to do if you get writer's block or write yourself into a corner. And how to review, revise, and rewrite the completed manuscript and how to sell it. He has quoted from the works of the top practitioners of genre writing and has presented examples of what not to do and why it should not be done.

John Stevenson tells you everything you need to know to write genre novels and break into print. He does all of this with a breezy, easy-to-read style with flashes of a keen sense of humor. Even if you needed to learn nothing from this book, I could recommend it as an interesting piece of literature. As it is, what you are holding in your hands is one of the clearest, most easily understood textbooks on fiction writing. If after reading this book you cannot write genre fiction and sell it on the open market, then writing is not your forte.

TONY HILLERMAN

Introduction

To those of us who have the ability to work with words, there are a number of avenues open: journalism, magazine articles, short stories, and the novel. Journalism and magazine articles deal with nonfiction and, as such, require a different approach than does fiction, where the writer can tailor the facts to suit the needs of his story. As a writer of fiction, your prime function is to manipulate the reader's vicarious feelings. Your main consideration should be to draw lifelike characters and steep them in plausible circumstances. Only when you can make the reader actually live the story you are setting down, and have exhorted the maximum empathy, will you have established your goal.

The different genres available to you vary mainly in the background material. Perhaps writing genre fiction could best be described as taking a good plot, peopling it with identifiable characters, and finding the ideal setting in which to place it. The same could be said of short stories (with one exception: a type of short story called a *mood piece* has no plot or theme and relies solely on the writer's skill with words to juggle the reader's emotions). As will be seen in the section devoted to plotting, it is far more than word count that makes up the difference between short stories and novels.

For most writers, a novel is a form of self-expression, frequently prescribed as a form of mental therapy. People writing novels can live their lives knowing that every day has a happy ending. It is the ultimate in fantasizing; let the psychiatrists make of it what they will. The writer can become each of the characters in turn, take on their personalities, indulge in all of their pleasures, and become heroic, cowardly, or defensive to show himself or herself in other guises in the best light.

As a writer of fiction, I know that I am not alone in this. Anybody who has purchased this book has the same interest at heart. There are other reasons why I should write genre fiction. Not the least of them is that my landlord comes visiting at frequent intervals, and I do get hungry. It is good for my health to eat from time to time. Also, like most people, I like to see my name in print; if this were my only consideration, I would be content with a listing in the telephone directory, but there is nothing to compare with the feeling you get when you hold your first book in your hands, knowing you have created every word of it.

The very first novel I wrote is still lying around somewhere. I have lost count of the rejection slips it earned—which is where this book comes in. Had I had access to the kind of book I am trying to write now, my first novel may have been a success. I learned from experience, which is time consuming and even less susceptible to guarantees than reading a book on the subject. That I have written a number of publishable novels does *not* mean that I have found some magical formula to write *successful* novels.

Perhaps I should define what I mean by *publishable* as opposed to *successful*. I consistently turn out novels that publishers consider sufficiently well-written, with enough appeal to the public, to offer me a contract and an advance. I consider these publishable. If I wrote books in the same class as Harold Robbins, Irving Wallace, Sidney Sheldon, and Judith Krantz, I would consider them successful. So maybe it's all a matter of the money one accepts. If I had found a magic formula to make my books publishable, I would be hard at work trying to find the formula that made *The Carpetbaggers, The Plot, Rage of Angels,* or *Princess Daisy* so financially successful. If there is one thing I like doing better than eating, it is eating well. And I would not mislead you by suggesting that Harold Robbins or Judith Krantz found a magic formula. Every book one writes is a unique experience, differing from the last one, just as it differs from the next one and the one after that, and so on, ad infinitum.

I have written a series of books all featuring the same protagonist. The only similarity among the books, however, is the personality of the lead character; in each, the plot and locale differ widely. I have also ghost-written books in the Sharpshooter series and several of the Nick Carters, which is a wonderful way to get practice for anybody getting started. Of course I could never get rich that way, but it pays the rent and puts groceries on the table.

Those kinds of books are definitely not written to a formula, although they do have a certain similarity to the story structure, but to find the magic formula I cannot recommend studying them in depth.

For one thing, such a series is written by a great number of writers, all of whom have their own ideas.

With your ability to paint word pictures, you have the power to transform the reader into the daring, swashbuckling idol of every right-thinking woman everywhere, or to make your reader the beautiful princess who is rescued by the dashing knight in armor and taken to his castle, no matter if the readers are approaching their hundredth birthday or are hospital-bound invalids who will never walk again. You can take a child's hand and lead that child through a world of magic, complete with talking animals and friendly flying dragons. The power that is yours is limitless. If your aim is to change the course of the world, the power is still yours, but your energy would be better directed to works of a political nature. If, like myself, you find a sense of accomplishment in taking a person on a trip of adventure, and for a few glorious hours making him or her (and yourself) the people we could never be, then this is the business for you.

Now I will let you in on my secret. I don't write to make money or to see my name in print, and I don't do it for any such altruistic reasons as giving pleasure to other people. I do it for me. I thoroughly enjoy these trips into the world of fantasy. If I can take my readers along with me, give them pleasure, and pay the rent in the process, I am a contented man.

When you are writing, you are trying to please the public, in the form of your publisher, but long before you can please anybody else, you have to please yourself. If I ever write a story that displeases me, I shall bury it because if I am not pleased with it, nobody else could be. With regard to my own work, I am easy to please.

The object of this book, then, is to provide a guide to those people who have a desire to write genre fiction, to break into print and get paid for it, based on my experiences and what I have learned from other writers during conversation and from their books. It goes without saying that there are no guarantees. Simply because you bought this manual and studied it diligently does not mean that you are going to write a number one best seller. Quite the reverse is true. If I were capable of turning out a number one best seller, I would not be spending my time writing a textbook like this. What this book contains is all the information I wish I had had available when I first started writing.

1.

Writing
Techniques

There are as many different writing techniques as there are writers. Since we do what we do for pleasure, one's techniques may be chosen by whim. If it feels comfortable, it must be right. To the fledgling writer, the urge to write is a basic necessity, whether it be seated at a desk in front of the latest model typewriter or squatting on one's heels with a stub of pencil and a notebook on some grassy slope. The drive is there, and if you deny it, you are doing yourself irreparable harm by stifling a natural impulse.

A great many of our more successful writers write countless drafts on the way to a completed manuscript. Among them are Sidney Sheldon, who wrote fourteen drafts of *The Other Side of Midnight*, and Colleen McCullough, who did ten drafts of *Thornbirds* on her way to the final presentation. On the other hand, other writers just do a light review at the time of creation before putting it through the typewriter for the final copy. In any event, learning to write a salable manuscript is a long process fraught with rejection slips. While learning his craft before he sold anything, John Creasey is alleged to have received in excess of 250 rejection slips. Although few can claim that number of turn-downs, we all have had our fair share.

The first prerequisite of good writing is that you must be comfortable. Whether you are a person whose thoughts flow freely when facing the keyboard of a typewriter or one who sits and chews the stub of a pencil in order to get the ideas flowing, you cannot express your thoughts unless you are comfortable. For a great many years I, like so many others, wrote at the kitchen table. Only in recent years have I graduated to a desk in a room set aside as an office. Back in those early years, I drove a taxi to pay the rent and to put the groceries on the table, and my writing had to be done after my day's work was over.

I cannot stress strongly enough the necessity to approach the writing life on a part-time basis. There is plenty of time to become a full-time writer; in the meantime, you need a regular paycheck to help you over the barrier of rejection slips and starvation. There is a completely erroneous idea that all one needs is talent in order to become a successful writer. Nothing could be further from the truth. It may take talent, but it also takes a certain amount of study and a great deal of hard work (and I have yet to meet a person who can accurately assess the degree of talent they have). Today's publishers are seeking writers who are ready to be published *today*, writers who know what to write and how to write it. And that doesn't come with talent, but only with study and practice.

To make the most of your gifts, you should approach writing as a job. The hours you put in at your task should be adjusted to suit your convenience, but once you have decided upon them, you should stick rigidly to your schedule. I know of several writers who dress every morning to give themselves the illusion of going to work. I take advantage of the fact that my office is only about ten feet away from my bedroom and frequently put in my first appearance of the day clad only in a bath towel.

Whether or not it is because of the days when I held a steady job in the daytime and habitually wrote only in the evening, I now find it almost impossible to write well in the morning. My best writing is always done at night. Normally I start writing at about four or five o'clock in the evening. After putting in a four- to eight-hour stint, I then invariably sleep until noon. Afternoons are spent taking care of my correspondence and reading. This is a schedule that I adhere to rigidly, and not just five days a week. I work seven days a week. Those hours suit me best. What I am advocating, then, is that you select your own hours—and abide by them.

Writing a book is a long, continuous process. By nature, a writer's life is a very lonely one, and it would help to be marooned on a desert island. Ideal as that may sound, it would have its drawbacks, like where would you plug in your electric typewriter? Everybody who knows me is familiar with my hours and knows enough not to call me except in the afternoon. The advantage of leading a normal family life is that you have somebody to answer the telephone or doorbell during your creative hours. Not having that advantage, I tend to be something less than patient with people ringing my doorbell before noon, and the best fifteen cents I shall ever spend is the sum the telephone company bills me every month for having an unlisted number.

I've found it advantageous to write at night, I have no view from the window to distract me at that time of night, children playing on the street are nonexistent, and I would much rather imagine my own stories than watch those on TV. Nor do I have to rearrange the furniture to make the most of the daylight. I have a fluorescent reading lamp that gives me all the light I need.

Although I invariably write my personal correspondence directly on the typewriter, I still handwrite my manuscripts with a ballpoint pen. Not being a very able typist, I find that I need to handwrite my books in order to keep up with my thoughts. The first chore of my working day is to proofread and correct the previous evening's work, then I type it. I find that daily proofreading keeps me clear of those repetitive words and phrases and helps to avoid redundancies. When I first started to write, I knew enough to avoid clichés, but I was prone to repeat words—a habit that daily proofreading seems to have cured.

I use a ballpoint pen on a yellow lined legal pad. One such fifty-sheet pad gives me about 12,500 words, which means that five such pads give me a 60,000-word novel. Above my desk is a shelf of reference books, most of which are common to every writer, but even in this I am not without idiosyncrasies. There are, of course, *Webster's Dictionary*, *Roget's Thesaurus*, *Hammond's Family Atlas*, and *Bartlett's Familiar Quotations*, and the *Elements of Style* by Strunk and White, although in all honesty I have read that little masterpiece so many times I almost have it committed to memory. What is peculiar to my own shelf of reference books is Berry and Van Den Bark's *American Thesaurus of Slang*, indispensable to anybody writing dialogue. It lists, for example, well over a hundred slang synonyms for *prostitute*. Also in residence on that shelf is Dean Grenell's *Pistol and Revolver Digest*, which tells me everything I may need to know about handguns. There are also French, Italian, and Spanish dictionaries. That may seem like a lot of dictionaries, but I keep the French because in the early stages of becoming a writer I translated and adapted several French suspense/romances for the American market. The Italian dictionary is there because most of the books I wrote under the name of Mark Denning were translated into Italian and sometimes the translators play fast and loose with my titles, as I did myself with the French books. The Spanish dictionary is there because my cleaning woman speaks no English.

Behind my chair, within easy reaching distance, is a set of encyclopedias and other reference books that are not in so much demand as the others. In the living room, far enough away not to tempt me, is the rest of my library, with the top shelf reserved for my books and those autographed books by other authors—the latter far outnumbering the former.

My writing day starts with proofreading the previous evening's work. After this I type and file it, keeping out the last page so that I can continue without losing the flow. Then I refer to my card system to refresh my mind on the scene, and I start writing. My card system is entered on 3 x 5" cards, one card for each chapter. These cards are filled out before I start working on the book and consist of cryptic sentences and phrases that outline the action made out from the working outline.

I use these cards simply as a rough guide, but one has to start somewhere. I find that this is enough to get me going. From what I have written on the card, I can visualize the scene and take note of the dialogue. There is nothing inflexible about either my card system or my story at this point. I can (and quite frequently do) change the subplots within the whole structure. I'll be talking about that at much greater length in the section devoted to plotting. All one needs to get started is a place to start and a place to finish. The subplots and the action along the way are all very tentative. A strong character might suggest a detour from the action you have mapped out, and it would be sheer foolishness to go ahead with any action not in keeping with the character's traits. If that piece of action is fundamental to your overall story, you may even find it necessary to go back and rewrite the character.

Now to discuss the actual writing. Once I have set the scene in my mind, I write without interruption for at least a couple of hours before I take a break for a snack or to replenish the ever-present scotch and soda. While I am actually writing, I stop for nothing. My spelling is usually good, but if there is any doubt in my mind, I wait to check the dictionary when I proofread.

I do the same thing with the thesaurus. The crucial point at this time is the flow. Once I have set the scene, I have an irresistible urge to get it down, and I cannot stop until I have it all out of my system. I begrudge the time it takes me to go into the kitchen to build myself a sandwich. My bar is in my office, which takes care of my inspiration.

Referring to the dictionary or the thesaurus is a time consuming delay that interferes with the flow of my thoughts. The success of my writing lies in its cadence. If I stop to check the spelling of a word or to look for a synonym, that interrupts the rhythm. Normally my spelling is fairly accurate, but a conscientious typist will always correct that for me on the final presentation; and in any case, very little gets past the proofreaders at the publishing house.

In the interest of saving time and keeping the flow going, I have sometimes used the same word as often as four or five times in one three-hundred-word page. These repetitions are glaringly obvious when I proofread the page, but at that time I have the leisure to refer to *Roget's Thesaurus* or *Webster's Synonyms* and select alternate words before typing the rough draft. My first draft is usually the same as the final presentation, unless I make a change in one of the subplots. Again, the key to my own good writing is comfort. I have a well-padded swivel chair, an ashtray, and a supply of cigarettes within easy reach. My proofreading is done with my feet on the desk and *Webster's* and *Roget's* at my elbow. After I have typed the first draft and filed it, only then do I place my feet squarely on the floor, hitch my chair up to the desk, and go to work. Once started, I continue until I reach an emotional break, which may or may not be the end of the chapter.

I try to do as much preplanning as possible. In advance I know just how much action there is going to be in any given chapter, and roughly how long that chapter will be. Even when my publisher calls for any story changes, it should not interfere with the plotting of the overall structure and the length of the chapters.

When I have finished the first rough draft, I proofread the entire book at one sitting, making minor corrections to rectify the rhythm of the words or to clarify situations. Like most prolific writers, I expect my work to be right the first time, and I have no patience with anybody who rewrites an entire book because of what they refer to as their perfectionism. This "perfectionism" is all too frequently an excuse for a lack of confidence. Like most authors, I can go back through some of my earlier works, published and unpublished, and pick out phrases that could be improved upon, but that is a needless and unending task.

Fortunately I had the courage of my convictions and submitted these earlier books. Had I not done so, I would still have been perfecting my first manuscript, pounding away at an old manual typewriter at the kitchen table, instead of leaning back in my padded swivel chair with an electric typewriter at my elbow and the money to pay a professional typist.

In the introduction I stated that I wrote genre novels for the sheer pleasure of it. Not that I would reject any attempt to pay me for my work. A hungry writer is not a good writer. One must be adequately nourished to do good writing. Of course you may feel more relaxed with an entirely different routine. You should mold your daily schedule to your taste. What I have outlined here is the schedule that suits me best. A great many people feel more competent writing in the morning, unlike "night people" like myself, and again, you may feel more comfortable creating directly onto the typewriter. All of this is a matter of personal choice. You are going to do it, so you decide.

I think it is a mistake to give up a full-time job in order to take up writing as a career. You owe it to yourself to prove that your efforts are not being wasted. It's nice to be so financially secure that you are able to devote all your time to writing, but anyone—especially a writer—needs a diversification of interests. I have outside hobbies that take me out of my office, and I would not have it any other way.

More often than not, I find myself hurrying to get back to work, because I find real-life situations frequently cannot compare with the make-believe world I create. A writer of fiction has the world at his fingertips—not the world as it is, but that Utopian world that is so desirable: That world where every person and every situation are logical; where even the so-called coincidence turns out to be the product of a rational situation or the end result of a positive action; where people come to logical conclusions and then act on them; and where every move is decisive.

In the writer's world, people have positive emotions and enact positive actions, unlike the real world where people sometimes delay their decisions and embrace the doctrine that a problem will go away if only they ignore it long enough. It is a world that you create to satisfy your whims: a world in which you play God, where every situation is of your own making, and everybody strictly abides by the principles you have created for them.

In order to create a perfect world and allow your readers to share in this paradise where you alone are God, you must be comfortable. There should be no gnawing hunger pangs in the stomach, no leaky roof dribbling raindrops down your neck. Instead, you should have your own version of peace and quiet.

Unlike many people today, I grew up in a world where portable radios had not been invented. When I was going to school, listening to the radio was an event. Each evening we used to gather around the family console for the family's entertainment. Having grown up in those circumstances, I find that any noise is distracting while I am trying to work. The only time I turn my radio on is when I go to bed; then I tune it to a radio station that plays "listening music." The only time I watch TV is for the news. It saddens me to think of how many children are physically incapable of doing their homework unless they have a radio at their side. I prefer to do without noise. It is, after all, a personal preference and I advise you to control the volume to a level that will enable you to do your best work.

It had been my intention to write about style, but on further consideration I believe that would be redundant. Obviously you have some writing skills, or you would not have selected this book. What could I say about style that William Strunk has not already said—and much better than I could say it? So turn the radio up, down, or off. Hitch your chair a little closer to the desk or kitchen table, and let's play God.

SELECTING
THE GENRE

2.

The
Various
Genres

You may be one of the few writers who is smitten with the idea of writing a novel at the same time that you realize what the story will be about. But it is more likely that the idea of writing a novel is comparatively fresh. You just haven't got around to deciding what the subject matter will be.

If you are graduating to novel writing from a successful period of short story writing, you will probably feel most comfortable with the same subject matter. If you have had some success with confession stories, you may find it easier to stay with contemporary romances. Perhaps you may have led an interesting life, and your novel might be based on your experiences as an arctic explorer. Or can you adapt your wartime experiences into your novel's plot? A great many first novels are autobiographical, with the majority of them being one-shot deals: But the exceptions are indeed outstanding ones. Dick Francis retired from his life as a steeplechase jockey to become one of the world's most popular mystery novelists, using horse racing as a background. Joseph Wambaugh is an ex-cop whose several police procedural books have made appearances on the best-seller list. Of course, it doesn't always work that way: Al Nussbaum was a bank robber until the FBI caught up with him, whereupon he spent quite a few years in the slammer. Al's talent for writing was not channeled into "Bonnie and Clyde" type stories about bank hold-ups or another prison life saga. Instead, he became a short story writer and literary critic.

If you enjoy reading romances and have a natural bent for history, you may feel more comfortable with historical or Regency romances: Why not combine success with confession stories and your natural talent for history to the same purpose? Similarly, an interest in the Old West with a little reading on the type of western fiction currently available at the newsstands could easily prepare you for a career in writing westerns.

I strongly advise you to write a few genre novels for practice before setting your sights on the best-seller list. The best-seller list varies from week to week, and the only thing it can do for you is to give you some idea of what formats are most popular at that particular time. By the time your book comes out, the entire picture may have changed. If you can write a genre novel of sufficient merit (which you will certainly not be able to do without a lot of practice), it will find its way on to the best-seller list.

You will have to do some research on the market opportunities for the various genres. There is nothing quite so fickle as the reading public and what is popular today may be quite passé next week. The *Writer's Market* gives information that is as up-to-date as possible within an annual publication on what particular categories of books the publishers are looking for. *Publisher's Weekly* and *Writer's Digest* keep track of the information on a weekly and monthly basis, and the Writer's Associations' monthly newsletters will frequently up-date market information. The only problem here is the time lapse: It takes time for a need in the market to make itself felt. For example, you may find there is a great demand for gothics and set about writing a gothic. Unless you are a very fast writer and can turn it out within a month—highly unlikely with your first novel—by the time you have it ready for the publisher, the demand will have gone, to be replaced by something else, perhaps westerns.

To my mind, the best approach is to select your genre and stay with it for several novels. In that way you will have a novel ready to submit to whichever publishers announce a requirement. And since publishers try to second-guess the reading public, there are always several publishers looking for the same type of novel at the same time, which gives you an alternative publisher should your first choice reject your manuscript.

Every writer is first and foremost a reader, and your first choice of reading matter will in all likelihood be the genre that you will be most comfortable writing. There are, of course, exceptions to that. I know of one lady who has had considerable success writing Regency romances whose favorite reading material is espionage novels, but she is the exception. I have not been able to figure out why she doesn't write an espionage novel set against a background of the Napoleonic wars (even if espionage was not generally recognized until 1939 when the term "fifth column" came into general usage).

If you take stock of the books that you have accumulated for light reading, you will find that your preference is quite obvious. Now, if you take a longer look at the ones you enjoyed the most, you will discover those that you feel were well within your writing capabilities. Once you have narrowed things down this far, go out and buy yourself a stack of books in that genre by a variety of different authors. Spend a full weekend reading them to narrow it down even further. You may find that you like espionage novels, but because you haven't travelled very much, feel that you should confine your locales to the continental United States. Or that you might prefer mysteries of the "locked-room" variety. In any event, recognizing your interests and abilities is the first step, and perhaps the most important one in becoming a genre novelist. Each genre is comprised of several subgenres. The next few chapters will be devoted to fully listing the alternatives, defining the categories as far as possible to give you the widest choice.

3.

Romances

Love has made the world go 'round since time began and will continue to do so until you and I are long past caring. So what better place to start your genre fiction writing than on the ground floor?

The basic romance story in its most simple form is *girl meets boy, girl loses boy, girl and boy are reunited and live happily ever after.* From there on, any number of intricacies make the story gradually more complex. The basic romance story is used as a subplot in almost all book-length fiction except for those wartime stories that have an exclusively male cast of characters, so before going on to the genre of your choice, it might be a good idea to get a good grasp of the principles involved. If you are aiming for the romance itself, you have five choices: the historical romance, the Regency, romance-suspense, the contemporary, and the gothic.

The historical romance takes place in any period of time and in any locale, from the Roman Empire up to fairly recent times. Basically it is a love story where the romance (and, usually, marriage) grows out of a shared experience. Depending on the era, there could be some overt violence (storming of the Bastille). The heroine is almost always young and virginal while the hero is strong, courageous, and thoroughly dependable.

Needless to say, if you are going to write an historical romance, you must be well versed in the history of that particular era and you must make the setting quite clear to the reader. In *Love's Avenging Heart* Patricia Matthews sets the time and the locale as well as introducing her heroine and her villain:

> On a summer morning in July 1717, early risers in the village of Williamsburg, Virginia were treated to the sight of a short, pudgy, ill-kempt man pulling a tall, buxom, red-headed lass of perhaps sixteen along the dusty streets, by a rope around her shapely neck.
>
> At the end of the rope, Hannah McCambridge, head held as high as the cruel tug of the rope would permit, fought back tears, and tried to ignore the stares and the snickers. Her hands were lashed together behind her back.
>
> The tears that scalded her eyes were caused mostly by anger. Of all the indignities that she had suffered at the hands of her stepfather, Silas Quint, this was the worst; the final insult.*

Not only has Ms. Matthews introduced her heroine and her villain, she has left no doubt in the reader's mind as to the where and when of all this.

I read quite recently that Ken Follet, author of *The Eye of the Needle*, considers himself to be an historical writer. *The Eye of the Needle* was set in Great Britain during World War II. Since I served in that war, I found it disconcerting to be classed as an historical artifact. So in my case, in order to be able to write an historical romance, I must know something about love and have a memory going back to my teen years, but for most of you neophyte writers, it will take the knowledge that you have absorbed by study of the era.

The Regency romance covers the period 1811-1820 (usually known as the Napoleonic), and British and French aristocracy lend a touch of glamour to the story. The heroines are always wealthy, titled ladies, or poor but proud nobility. These were times of elegance and refinement, which should be reflected in the characters' way of life. The political situation may serve as a background; there is no violence, and the plots are light-hearted. One thing common to all romances is that the heroine dislikes the hero at first. In these books, there is no such thing as love at first sight. The characters need the full length of the book to sort out their feelings for each other.

Romance-suspense novels are those in which the main story or plot is girl meets boy, girl loses (or hates) boy, girl and boy are reunited and realize just how much they love each other. This is interwoven with a subplot of adventure—something like a cache of stolen jewels or perhaps an unjust accusation of some serious crime. Perhaps the father of the heroine has been wrongly accused of treason or some such

*From *Love's Avenging Heart* by Patricia Matthews. Copyright © 1976 by Patricia Matthews. Reprinted with permission of Pinnacle Books, Inc. and the author.

horrific crime casting aspersions on his ethics. In this case, the hero starts off by being on the other side but is won over by the heroine's honorable behavior. There is usually a second couple who are the perpetrators of the crime, and although they start off as the fiancé and fiancée of the lead couple, as the book draws to its conclusion their true colors show through. At the end, the lead couple gets married while the other couple (if they are still alive) are carted off to jail. Accidents are very prone to happen to these villains, and the second female lead is usually the brains behind the evil scheme, while her handsome counterpart supplies the brawn. Although the first lead couple acts in a most moral fashion, it is not unknown for the second couple to get caught in bed—just in case the reader didn't know whose side to be on. *The contemporary romance*, as the name implies, is a story set in current times. The operative word here is *current* and you must not inadvertently set a time on it by referring to the wars in Korea or Vietnam or landing men on the moon except as a point in history.

In other words you may not say, "now that Vincent had been back from Vietnam for a full year." Permissible is the much looser dating of the times such as, "our first year of college just before the boys came back from Vietnam."

However, contemporary romances must move with the times, and today's heroines can be older and wiser, perhaps even divorced, as opposed to teen-aged virgins. More graphic descriptions of sex can frequently be found, although the extent to which you use sex in your novels and the way in which you describe it are strictly matters of taste and should be settled between yourself and your editor. It is not unlikely that your divorced or widowed heroine might be a mother. The main point of the story is the love she feels for the hero, and he for her. After all, a great many of your readers will be mothers themselves, and if divorced, they too may still be looking for their one great love.

The gothic romance is more of a mood piece than any other genre; the mood it creates is one of a nebulous threat. The heroine goes to live at some remote house on the English moors to work as a governess, housekeeper, maybe even a nurse. She is young, beautiful, and virginal and attracts the attention of two men, the least likely of whom will turn out to be the villian. The other will turn out to be the second son of a Duke (or some such aristocrat) incognito or hiding out—and will be the man with whom she falls in love. The gothic romance can get very close to the occult, with such trappings as ghostly sightings (the ghosts are often real), rattling chains, and moans emanating from empty rooms.

Although the gothic is quite often set in the present, I person-ally think it adds to the ghostly atmosphere to set it back in Victorian times.

4.

Suspense and Western

Suspense novels are in a class all their own and concern themselves less with the action (whether it be romantic or more violent) than with the implied threat of menace to come. This makes the mood to be set all-important to the tone of the entire novel. In fact, a good suspense novel will start by painting a picture of mood into which the suspense can be set.

Brian Garfield opens his novel, *Hopscotch,* as follows:

> In Paris the gambling was hidden but easy enough to find. This one was in the fifteenth arrondissement near the Citroën factory. The thick door had an iron ring for a handle; a thug absurdly disguised as a doorman admitted Kendig and there was a woman at a desk, attractive enough but she had a cool hard air. Kendig went through the tedium of establishing the credentials of his innocence—he was not a *flic,* he was not Sicilian, he was not Union Corse, he was not this or that. "Just a tourist. I've been here before with Mme. Labrie. There isn't a message for me by any chance?"
>
> There wasn't. Kendig paid the membership admission and crossed to the elevator. *There will be an interesting message for you tonight at the Club Rouge.* It had been typed, no signature; delivered to his *concierge* by an urchin clutching a five-franc note.
>
> He went up in a lift cage piloted by a little fellow whose face was the texture of old rubber dried grey by a desert sun: the look of an Algerian veteran. The old fellow opened the gate on the third étage. "*Bonne chance, M'sieur.*" Behind the smile was a leering cynicism.
>
> Kendig's fathomless eyes looked past the tables at a desolate emptiness of his own. The crowd was moderate, the decor

discreet, the costumery tiresomely fashionable. Soft laughter here, hard silence there: winners and losers. The bright lighting leeched their faces of color. Kendig drifted among the felted tables. A croupier recognized him from somewhere and smiled; he was in the uniform—the tuxedo that only appeared to have pockets; to discourage temptation. Kendig said, "They've moved the poker?"

"You must speak with the *maître*." The croupier glanced toward a largish man in black who loomed over the neighboring wheel.

Kendig had a word with the *maître* and had to show his bankroll to the cashier behind a cage. He bought five thousand francs in rectangular chips and the *maître* guided him officiously past the tables to an oak door with massive polished brass fittings. Beyond it Kendig found the game.*

This sets an air of sinister menace where anything can happen. As Mr. Garfield says, "One should not confuse violence with suspense. When violence starts, suspense ends."

The time period of the suspense novel is usually contemporary, although there is no hard-and-fast rule, and I am quite sure that some great suspense novels could have been set in the times of Frankenstein or Count Dracula's Transylvania. As in almost all fiction, the time the writer is living in imparts an aura of feasibility to the scenes with the exception of historical novels and westerns.

Dashiell Hammett set many of his short stories and five novels in the Prohibition era. Could Nick and Nora Charles have been brought so vividly to life if *The Thin Man* had been written in the forties or fifties? Raymond Chandler's novels, set in the forties, are generally regarded as masterpieces of current literature. Could he have created his characters and settings with the same flavor ten or twenty years later?

But to look at it from your own point of view as a new writer about to get started, the times you are living in and the locales you are familiar with are perhaps the most important aspects that you will bring to your story.

There is no standard plot for the suspense novel. By its very definition, the story deals with what *might* happen, and the degree of success you may attain with this genre depends on the plausibility of the implied threats. In most cases the implied threat is canceled out by a token amount of violence at the end of the book, but this does not mean that you are not successful in writing the suspense novel. The various genres borrow heavily from each other without destroying their

*From *Hopscotch* by Brian Garfield. Copyright © 1975 by Brian Garfield. Reprinted by permission of the author, the publisher, M. Evans and Company, Inc., New York, New York 10017, and the JCA Literary Agency, Inc.

main purpose. Where would a contemporary novel be without a romantic interest, or an historical romance without a sword fight?

The main plot can be one of extortion, the threat of a ship sinking far from land, or the old stand-by of the new bride who has reason to believe that her husband is a psychopathic killer. The choice is endless; the only thing you are unlikely to do is find something new. More about plotting later.

The *western* is one of the oldest of the genre novels, dating back before the times of the mystery stories, the classic Sherlock Holmes "Whodunit."

It is set in the last half of the nineteenth century, in one of the western states, naturally, and reflects a very important part of this country's growth. The protagonist is invariably a "loner," quite frequently a stranger to the parts where the action takes place.

The story usually involves an unscrupulous rancher intent on adding to his herds or to his grazing lands, or an equally unscrupulous railroad owner bent on accumulating land for his railroad that nobody wants anyway.

There is a very strict code of ethics in these books. It is not unknown for the protagonist to marry the widowed rancher, who is the target of the villain, but there are no lovemaking scenes and definitely no sex. Sometimes the protagonist will make friends with one of the dance hall girls, but she is never to be referred to as, or even implied that she might be, a whore. There are times, when studying this country's literature, I find it difficult to understand why this nation's population didn't come to a screeching halt about the time of the Naughty Nineties.

A very popular subplot (or alternatively, a main plot with a greedy rancher or railroad owner as the subplot) is the man seeking vengeance for the murder of his parents or his sheriff brother. Every western hero is an expert shot, and very fast on the draw, and his parents or his sheriff brother were shot in the back. But *he* never shoots anyone in the back, and he always lets the other guy have the first shot. His parents may have been killed by arrows and scalped by renegades masquerading as Indians; this last premise will require some knowledge of Indian tribal customs in order to bring the villains to justice.

A good western cannot be written without a knowledge of the country and customs of the time, in particular the flora and fauna of the area you intend to write about. Since your main character is an outdoorsman, put your cacti in the right places, and make sure you know how to groom a horse before you start describing how your protagonist does it.

The very popular ambush—an historical fact of the times practiced by outlaws—sticks to its own rigid code. The outlaws representing the villains of the stories have no compunction about shooting unarmed men and kidnapping defenseless women. But since even the villains are pure of thought and will turn their heads when their captives bathe in streams, I cannot see much point in the kidnapping. It certainly did very little to counteract the under-population that was a sign of the times.

Perhaps the "Wild West" could be likened to the cowboys and Indians games we used to play before we found that girls were different from boys (and why). The usual western has considerable violence in the form of gunplay and not a few fist fights, but no gory descriptions of what happens if a guy gets shot in the head with a .45 Colt. It's all good, clean fun, like the ever-popular western movies that only appear on late night TV.

5.

Occult
and
Action-Adventure

The *occult* story has features in common with both the suspense and action/adventure genres. There is considerable suspense while the protagonists (usually a man and his wife) are haunted or visited by some unknown force, and a great deal of violence while the force—now recognized for what it is—makes itself felt, building to a climax as they finally rid themselves of it. These stories are often called *horror* stories, which may more clearly define the genre, and it takes a great amount of creativity to leave behind the legendary myths like vampires or the Devil who appeared to sire *Rosemary's Baby* and to come up with something new, as Stephen King did in his *Firestarter.*

The plot normally is one in which a man and his wife go to live in an old home (it helps the suspense along if the house has stood empty for some time because the natives of the area are afraid of its bogyman), and they very soon find evidence of some evil spirit sharing the house with them. When the full impact of the happenings occurs to them, they take steps to rid themselves of it. In *The Howling,* Gary Brandner took his protagonists from a mood of complete relaxation into a suspenseful aura of implied menace with this passage:

> Laughing together, they continued up to the front stoop. Roy stood aside and gestured her into the living room.
> Karyn started in, then hesitated. She ran her fingers down the surface of the heavy wooden door. Under the fresh green paint a series of vertical grooves like scars slashed the panel at about shoulder height.
> "What do you suppose made these?" she said.
> "Who knows?" Roy shrugged and went on inside.

> Karyn followed, thinking about the marks. Absurd though it
> was, the angry furrows in the wood suggested only one thing.
> Claws.*

That one word, *claws*, is perhaps one of the finest examples I
have ever seen of a prognosis of horror yet to come. There is nothing yet
to frighten the protagonists: In fact, they treat it very casually, but it is
designed to scare the hell out of the reader, which is what the whole
genre is about.

The horror story can date the time of its birth to Mary Shelley's
Frankenstein in 1818. Although Robert Louis Stevenson (no relation)
produced *Dr. Jekyll and Mr. Hyde* in 1886, the horror story did not
become popular as a genre until quite recently. In the meantime, the
subject has been material for numerous movies with very good reason.
It takes an accomplished writer to match the horror of a movie set in—
as an example—a waxworks museum, while special effects in movies
have long known how to make an ethereal body appear at will.

Occult stories have only just come into their own as an
independent genre and, as the youngest genre, it may well be where the
greatest opportunity lies.

Action-Adventure books make full use of fast action and violence not
only in the setting of the problem but also in its resolution. They are
roughly divided into four separate subgenres: the espionage novel, the
straight adventure, the wartime, and the series. The *espionage* deals
with the purloining of state secrets with the inherent death sentence;
the *straight adventure* novel deals with safaris into unexplored territory
to seek hidden treasures and other such exotic experiences; the *wartime*
story can deal with any war as long as the protagonist is on the side of
the angels (although World War II was the most popular war we have
had, and the Nazis the most popular villains); and the *series* novel
features a man with a mission and is usually enacted within the
continental United States. Again, there can be considerable overlap
between the different subgenres, and the protagonist can be an official
directed to the operation by his superior or an innocent bystander who
witnesses something that offends his sense of justice or who is drawn
into the plot against his will, as in most Alfred Hitchcock stories.

The basic plot is the presentation of the problem, which on the
surface appears to have a simple solution. As the protagonist starts to
take action, the simple solution becomes gradually more complex until
he is faced with a world holocaust and until with one stroke of genius
disaster is averted and the problem solved. International espionage and

*From *The Howling* by Gary Brandner (Fawcett, 1976). Reprinted by permission of the author.

counterespionage provide such good motivation for fast action and violence that it is not surprising that the other subgenres borrow heavily from it, even the series. The basic espionage novel can only be set in some other country frequently used as a catspaw by some all-powerful world power, while the counterespionage story is set in the States and involves preventing other people from doing to us what we are doing to them. Not unusual is the espionage story where a tourist is approached by the CIA (perhaps a dying agent) to transport microfilm of world-shattering importance. The straight adventure tale deals, once again, with action abroad—perhaps a shipwreck, although I don't think there are any undiscovered islands in the South Pacific and nowhere else would it be warm enough to live without supplies of water and fresh game. Or, depending on your knowledge, you might be able to write a plausible story with a background of mountaineering in the Swiss Alps—an avalanche could be most climactic, or getting lost in the desert—either the Sahara or the great Sandy Desert in Australia.

Stories of World War II always seem to be in demand although (as I have pointed out elsewhere in this book) even though it was our most popular war, memories of it are fading and now, unless you are a senior citizen, it takes a certain amount of study to keep your facts straight. The series novels can be separated by their protagonists' motivations. On one hand is the "Executioner" written by Don Pendleton, perhaps the most successful of all the series, and the "Sharpshooter". Here both protagonists' motivations are all-out war against the Mafia. Opposed to them is Nick Carter, written by a whole stableful of writers, the longest running series of all (would you believe since 1886?), and Matt Helm written by Donald Hamilton, both of whom work for some secret Federal Agency and whose work consists of espionage, counterespionage, and terrorist repression. The Mafia type usually, although not always, has a locale in the continental United States, while Nick Carter books are more often than not set in some exotic background. I have written some of these myself, using Singapore and Australia as a backdrop.

Violence is the stock in trade of all action/adventure stories although certainly not limited to them. It is the hub about which the whole story revolves: The action starts in the first few paragraphs and does not let go until the protagonist stands alone and unharmed. You are not looking at just violence, but at increasingly tense situations that can only be resolved with violence.

When I asked Don Pendleton about introducing violence into his *Executioner* series books he told me, "I usually open my books with my man in a tight situation which demands immediate action. However, action without dimension cannot be dramatic so I make it a point to background the opening scenes with a brief prologue which hopefully suggests the deeper dimensions of the conflict. For *Hawaiian Hellground* I sent Bolan first to Honolulu's national cemetery (The Punchbowl) for an identification with national purpose, duty, honor, etc...."

> He'd come to the Punchbowl simply to commune awhile with his dead brothers, to say 'hello' and 'goodbye'—and perhaps to remind himself that Mack Bolan also lay there, in effect if not in fact. All that had held meaning to the life of Mack Bolan had indeed ceased to exist many hard battles ago. All that was left was the mission itself and the hardcase warrior whom the entire world had come to know as the Executioner.... Every cop in the western world wanted his hide. The entire world of organized crime wanted his head—the bounties for which had now pyramided to a half-million bloody bucks. Several times he had been tempted to check it in, to let it go, to resign the mission and life itself. It could be so damned easy. Just let go. Just relax the vigil, for so much as a heartbeat—and, yeah, that heart would never beat again. But it was also hard for Mack Bolan to die. There was a job to be done. He was probably the only man living who had even an outside chance to do that job. So, sure, it was harder to die than to live. Life was for living, and a guy lived the hand that was dealt him. Those men beneath those crosses down there—they'd lived their hand to the bitter end. Mack Bolan could do no less.
>
> "I consecrate you," he quietly told them, then the Executioner went down to meet the enemy.*

The *series novels* are not to be confused with sagas. The series novels recount the adventures of one man in current times, whereas the saga tells of the (mis)adventures of an entire family throughout succeeding generations and is more in the form of mainstream fiction than of a specific genre.

*From *Hawaiian Hellground* by Don Pendleton. Copyright © 1975 by Pinnacle Books, Inc. Reprinted with permission of Pinnacle Books, Inc. and the author.

6.

Mystery
and
Science Fiction

Mystery stories also come in different subgenres: There are the police procedural, the private eye or newspaper reporter, and the innocent bystander. A completely different set of subgenre is that used by the publishing houses: the locked-room puzzle, the drawing room mystery, and hard-boiled P.I.

The *police procedural* is the mystery where a homicide is turned over to a squad of detectives to solve. A true police procedural, such as the ones that Joseph Wambaugh writes, cannot be written without an in-depth knowledge of actual police methods and forensic sciences. A lesser type of police procedural is the one where an investigator is arbitrarily given a police rank. All this does is to provide a convenience for the writer who can draw upon imaginary sources of research with little basis in fact. The private eye, newspaper reporter, and the innocent bystander have a great deal in common insofar as the stories themselves are concerned. Similar in investigation techniques, they differ in that the P.I. and the newspaper reporter get paid for their time and expenses, whereas the innocent bystander always finishes up out of pocket, a fact which has always struck me as stretching plausibility too far.

In the other subgenres, the locked-room puzzle presents a mystery where a dead body is found in a room with no method of exit for the murderer. The room has no windows or only windows that are heavily barred. The dead man has the only key in his pocket, and there is no booby trap such as a shotgun primed to fire when the safe door is opened, the recoils of the gun automatically closing the safe door. The drawing room mystery is a British concoction where all the people are aristocrats or upper middle class. It is so named because the investigation takes place during gatherings where all parties concerned sit around and drink tea and eat cucumber sandwiches. This subgenre is actually a psychological study of the characters entailed. The hard-boiled Private Investigator is easily recognized by his tough-talking attitude and his amoral conduct. Despite his attitude he has a very strong code of ethics, and he is known to associate with the criminal element unlike other investigators. The hard-boiled P.I. was introduced by Dashiell Hammett, picked up by Raymond Chandler, and continued by Mickey Spillane. But do not let the tough line of conversation fool you. All of these gentlemen mentioned are exceptionally fine writers as a cursory glance through their works will reveal. I cannot leave the area of the Private Investigator without mentioning that of all the P.I. novels, those written by Dashiell Hammett and Joe Gores warrant particular attention since both of these writers were once private investigators themselves, and their works have a feasibility seldom found elsewhere.

The mystery story, no matter what the subgenre, conforms to a standard formula. The entire book is taken up with the protagonist's inquiry into the circumstances surrounding the death of a person. As he follows up each clue, the solution keeps getting further away, and an increasing number of red herrings strewn in his path and quite often several more murders along the way build up to a climax where, depending on the subgenre, the investigator himself may be put in mortal danger. Naturally, the villain is exposed at the end and either confesses and is arrested, commits suicide, or suffers a fatal accident while trying to escape.

The plotting is far more complicated than in any other genre and each clue must be made to reveal no more than a certain amount. A great many writers, old pros and neophytes alike, dispense with a detailed plotting system, relying on their characterization, allowing themselves to follow their characters wherever they tend to lead them. This may work for some genres, but definitely *not* for the murder mystery where everything must have a definite purpose in the scheme of things.

Writing a murder mystery takes almost as much detailed research as writing a textbook on writing genre fiction, and although I rarely write mysteries except in short story form now, it is still my favorite choice of reading.

Science fiction novels are a breed apart, and not until the word *fantasy* gets tagged on to the genre title do we see any duplication in efforts. Most of the principles I covered under the heading of *occult* apply to the heading of fantasy, which can perhaps be best described as plain old scary stories. I have yet to meet a writer who will go out on a limb to give me a definition that I can quote in print. To me, fantasy is the world of fairies, elves, leprechauns and Tolkien's Middle Earth, and I intend to go on that assumption.

Science fiction is far easier to define. Science fiction stories take place at some time or place that we have yet to reach, and the plot detailing is as meticulous as is that of the mystery story. Science fiction is taking a look into the future and the advances that science will have made by that time. Interplanetary travel may come into it, but not necessarily. Your story could deal with people here on earth as long as they fit into the scientific development that we can expect by that time. The meticulous plotting comes in making sure that everything is in line with your fictionalized scientific advances.

As with the historical novel, it is of paramount importance to set the time and locale as an indication of what readers can expect of the scientific developments. In *West of Honor*, Jerry Pournelle opens his story with 2064 AD:

> The bright future she sang of was already stiffened in blood, but Kathryn Malcolm didn't know that, any more than she knew that the sun was orange-red and too bright, or that the gravity was too low.
>
> She had lived all of her sixteen standard years on Arrarat, and although her grandfather often spoke of Earth, humanity's birthplace was no home to her. Earth was a place of machines and concrete roads and automobiles and great cities, a place where people crowded together far from the land. When she thought of Earth at all, it seemed an ugly place, hardly fit for people to live on.
>
> Mostly she wondered how Earth would smell. With all those people huddled together—certaintly it must be different from Arrarat. She inhaled deeply, filling her lungs with the pleasing smell of newly turned soil. The land here was good. It felt right beneath her feet. Dark and crumbly, moist enough to take hold of the seeds and nurture them, but not wet and full of clods: good land, perfect land for the late-season crop she was planting.
>
> She walked steadily behind the plow, using a long whip to guide the oxen. She flicked the whip near the leaders, but never close enough to touch them. There was no need for that. Horace and Star knew what she wanted. The whip guided them and assured that she was watching, but they knew the spiral path as well as she did. The plow turned the soil inward so that the center of the field would be higher than the edges. That helped to drain the field and made it easier to harvest two crops each year.
>
> The early harvest was already gathered into the stone barn. Wheat and corn, genetically adapted for Arrarat: and in

29

another part of the barn were Arrarat's native breadfruit melons, full of sugar and ready to begin fermentation. It had been a good year, with more than enough for the family to eat. There would be a surplus to sell in town, and Kathryn's mother had promised to buy a bolt of printed cloth for a new dress that Kathryn could wear for Emil.

At the moment, though, she wore coveralls and high boots, and she was glad enough that Emil couldn't see her. He should know that she could plow as straight a furrow as any man, and that she could ride as well as her brother—but knowing it and seeing her here on the fields were two different things entirely, and she was glad that he couldn't see her just now. She laughed at herself when she thought this, but that didn't stop the thoughts.

She twitched the whip to move the oxen slightly outward, then frowned imperceptibly. The second pair in the string had never pulled a wagon across the plains, and Kathryn thought she could no longer put off their training. Emil would not want to live with Kathryn's grandfather. A man wanted land of his own, even though there were more than a thousand hectares in the Malcolm station.*

In a letter, Dr. Pournelle writes, "the historical writer can set century and place with the expectation that the reader will know something of what's going on. The science fiction craftsman can't expect that much. Language, atmosphere, social conditions—all these are variables. If the reader is left confused—as some writers seem to think desirable—he will abandon the book. Dedicated fans will hang on in confusion longer than the casual reader, but even they have their limits."

The time in *West of Honor* is some eighty years from now and takes place where agriculture is apparently a most important part of life. This ideally sets the time and place and introduces the first of his characters. This is obviously not going to be another *Star Wars* story of Muppet-type characters fighting space wars at faster than the speed of light. In his opening paragraphs, he has set his scene to the point where we really don't care very much what year it is. This is as it should be; once the reader has a firm grasp on the scientific developments that are available to the characters, actual time is irrelevant.

We could write a story about a disaster-filled hunting trip where all the hunters are using spears and clubs; from that context it might be important that the hunters will use fire to cook their food and animal skins to dress themselves—but the fact of its being the fourth or fifth century BC becomes totally immaterial. For that matter it could be

*From *West of Honor* by Jerry Pournelle. Copyright © 1978 by Jerry Pournelle. Reprinted by permission of the author, Pocket Books, a Simon & Schuster division of Gulf & Western Corporation, and Blassingame, McCauley and Wood.

twentieth century Australia or New Guinea, except that in both of those locations the climate is such that any form of dress is extraneous.

There are no limitations to your story. It could be a tale of pioneers trying to find a new planet to settle from an overcrowded Earth and their adventures along the way, bearing in mind that BEMs (Bug-eyed Monsters) are now passé. Or it could be a story of domestic simplicity here on earth, with such things as international currency, World Government, and local travel by light beams. Or you might want to write a good old-fashioned love story in a futuristic setting. I very much doubt if sex is going to become anachronistic no matter how much we avail ourselves of it. The one thing that you must avoid at all costs is the temptation to throw in some gimmick at the last moment, which is not in keeping with the rest of the scientific development, simply to supply the reader with a neat ending.

When it comes to fantasy, as in all other genres, you must beware of trite situations. Any writer worthy of the name is aware of trite words and phrases, but trite situations have a way of slipping past without that fresh approach that would make them distinctive. You might do a story on a research journalist investigating medieval sorcery who comes across a formula for making a genie appear: In the end, of course, he will disappear permanently because he cannot cope with modern living—sort of a science fiction tale in reverse. Or you might want to write a tale about a young couple who accidentally backpack into the long–lost land of nursery rhymes, complete with Jack and the Beanstalk, the House that Jack Built, et al. Trouble is, the only reason I can think of that the land remained undiscovered for so long is the enormous deposits of lodestone that deflect all compasses—which in itself is bordering on a trite situation.

THE
PLOT

7.

The
Story

The story is a sequence of events, not necessarily in chronological order, but arranged to reach the desired conclusion based on the overall theme. The author's aim is to arouse interest in the story by stirring the reader's curiosity—to keep him turning the pages. Related incidents keep leading him toward a conclusion, despite the contradictions that in effect do little but build up the final climax, which may be unexpected or inevitable. A story may develop from an interesting character, situation, idea, or even a title. Once you have the reader interested in the primary situation, you must keep the narrative flowing to maintain that interest. Only the author is in command of the story, keeping the reader trying to unravel the complexities that he finds strewn along his path to wherever the author wants to lead him in the final scheme of things. Without a story, we could no doubt settle it for the reader all at once, but a simple explanation is not literature. The story must create suspense no matter what the genre. The reader must want to know what happens next.

The one thing that I have not yet touched upon is that the genre book must be fun to write. A living can be made from writing genre fiction, but if you do not enjoy your work, you might as well engage in some other uninspired and menial task. When I found that I was able to earn a living writing genre fiction I felt that I had reached a milestone in my career, despite the inherent problems that came with it—like no paid vacation, no sick pay, and slow-paying publishers. I was able to overcome these hassles by looking upon them as an added spur to my output. Being one's own master and arranging one's hours to suit oneself, and deciding when to write and about what and for how long can be surpassed only by the enjoyment of the actual writing. So let's add enjoyment to the consideration of the final selection of the genre.

There are three stages in preparing your novel to be committed to the typewriter. First comes gathering the material—which in this case includes choosing the genre and selecting the background experiences you will be using. Second comes contemplation of the idea expressed as an overall theme, and third, selecting the motivation of the characters so that your people do what seems to be the most logical thing in any given circumstances.

I have given you all the subgenres from which you will make your choice. The selection itself is up to you; but if I talk about gathering the material you are going to use, it may make the choice easier. If you happen to be a retired arctic explorer contemplating a choice between writing a book or playing snowballs with the neighborhood kids, the choice will be obvious. A great many fiction writers have a long list of personal accomplishments: Jack London had been an oyster pirate, seaman, and hobo, and Ernest K. Gann has been a fisherman working out of San Francisco and an airline pilot. But it is not absolutely necessary to have a long list of personal experiences before you can write a book. Instead, you can simply put your imagination to work for you. This is what is known as playing "what if. . . ."

Before you can start playing "what if? . . . " your mind must be receptive to ideas—a condition that comes about through constant reading. You can use "what if? . . . " for forming ideas for a theme or for filling in the overall story line with situations. It can be done anywhere at any time, and all it consists of is taking note of the situations around you and allowing your imagination to work with them. The more mundane the situations, the better, and you might be surprised at what the most normal situations can suggest to you.

Have you ever seen a little girl crying on a street corner? What potential emotion you can find there! In reality she may have just dropped her ice cream cone, or she left her favorite doll on the seat of the car when a neighbor drove her home from school. But what if it were a real tragedy? Maybe she was kidnapped, made her escape, and now can't find her way home. Or did she see a murder committed, and is now afraid that the murderer is chasing her? The exercise in creativity comes when you ask yourself what *has* happened—and what is going to happen next.

The more I think about that example, the more I like it. What kind of story could not use a situation, a subplot, or even a complete theme around that child crying? She could be crying tears of joy because she just learned that she is going to see her father for the first time in several years. Or you can develop that even further. Her father doesn't show up, and in his failure to show up, there is another complete plot twist.

You will find that the reading you have been doing will guide your thoughts. If ou choose the romance school, there have been many tragic stories with children abandoned after a married couple separates. Should you favor the historical romance, that little girl is probably the crown princess of some small European country, kidnapped by wandering gypsies, finally making her escape in your home town (although how they crossed the Atlantic is for you to figure out). Maybe she is the daughter of an exiled ruler who came to America just one step ahead of the revolutionaries? Then your story can be how she befriends the Loyalist group here in America, and how they restore her to the throne.

Any time you walk down the street you can find a dozen stories on every block. You see a dog running down the street by himself: What opportunities are in that one? Ignore for a moment the possibilities of its being another Lassie on the way to rescue somebody. Is the dog lost? Just late for lunch? Maybe she belongs to a little girl, and what poignancy can be dredged up from that! The little girl is dying from some unkown fever, and the reunion with her dog wreaks a miraculous cure by restoring her will to live.

I live in an apartment building, and several of my neighbors have cats. One of these is a tabby named Tiger, and I know that if I walk outside he will come up and rub himself on my ankles. A very friendly cat, is Tiger, which gives me a story right there. How about a Tiger who can fly and is in the habit of flying to a wonderful land where all sorts of magical things can happen? Another of my neighbors has a Siamese cat, and every night at about five o'clock he climbs onto the window sill to wait for his mistress, glaring balefully at everybody who walks past. (Do Siamese cats ever glare any other way?) Or a different idea that comes to mind is to use the cat as the narrator of the story: romance, murder mystery or what-have-you. There are untold opportunities for humor here if we tell the story as seen through the cat's eyes, putting a feline interpretation on all the most human of the actions. What immediately comes to mind is:

> Tippy stretched herself, yawned, and went back to watching the peculiar human ritual going on before her. Why do people insist on submerging themselves in water? Tippy tried it once when she fell into the bird bath and swore she would never try it again. And then to dunk all that evil-smelling gunk all over themselves. Why on earth couldn't people use some pleasant-smelling stuff, like essence of liver? Tippy yawned again, closed her eyes and fell asleep.

That is only one paragraph, of course, but it should give you the idea, and it should not be too difficult to develop it into a theme for a novel. It would certainly be a different approach from the usual run of genre novels. It might also be well to note that it would make no difference to the basic story, which would still be in the same genre, but that we have changed the point of view. In the section on characterization, I cover the different points of view: first person, third person, and multiple or omniscient. When I wrote that, it never occurred to me that the first person could be a cat. As a matter of fact, had I thought of it earlier, I would have already used the idea. I *still* might: There is nothing to say that the first, or third person, whichever you decide to use to tell the story, must not be a cat. It could even be a polar bear should you so desire, but a cat has more contact with people, and it is far easier to imagine yourself lying on a shelf watching all the interchanges between the people you are writing about. I'll even give you a title, *The Catnappers*, which will more or less obligate you to use kidnapping as a central theme. Perhaps the cat might be a very rare species or a champion at cat shows, well worth kidnapping. To keep up the humor, the kidnapper hates cats or is afraid of them and the cat misinterprets every action as a gesture of friendship—extending the paw of friendship. You might even like to make the cat believe he is being taken away to perform stud services, and the disappointment he feels when there is no receptive female waiting for him.

What I have described here is a comedy—a genre that I have not listed earlier for the reason that comedy is not a genre in itself but more of a style of writing. *The Catnappers* would in effect be a suspense story written in a humorous style.

Let's take a title for the inspiration for your novel. We have just looked at the idea of developing a theme from the title of kidnapping a cat, seen from the cat's eyes. Let's see what other titles will do for your inspiration. Taking a look at romances, love is a common word to find in a title: In the chapter devoted to selecting the genre, I quoted from Patricia Matthews's *Love's Avenging Heart*. Rather than run the risk of duplicating somebody else's title, let's use the word *ardor*. Write the word *ardor* on a sheet of paper and see how many titles you can come up with using *ardor*: *Ardor Awakened; Ardor in Spring/Summer/Fall/Winter; Ardor Aroused; Ardor Bestirred; The Ardor of Anne*.

Stop when you find something that appeals to you and that suggests a theme.

You can do the same for westerns using the hyphenated words *shoot-out* and *six-gun*: *Shoot-Out at Copper Creek; Shoot-Out under the Hanging Tree; The Vengeance Shoot-Out; Six-Guns of the Plains; Shelley's Six-guns; Six-Guns and Aces*. Or the espionage stories: *The Spy who Slept; The Spy from New Jersey; Havana Spy; Spy from Reno*.

With adventure stories: *A Bullet for Bernie; Bullets and Bacchanalia; Bullets from Boston*.

I expect that by the time you have written a dozen titles in the genre you have been concentrating on, one of them will suggest a story to you. It may suggest a place to start, and since we already know where that genre will finish, it should not be too difficult to fill in the rest of the skeleton outline of the plot.

The skeleton of the plot must be based on an apparently minor problem that the protagonist is faced with at the outset of the book. Each attempt to solve it is unsuccessful and only manages to worsen the situation until the obstacle is insurmountable. Finally he finds the solution through ingenuity, courage, or doggedness.

Sub-plots can be interwoven throughout the book, tying in with the main plot at the end, no matter how unrelated they appear to be. Example: Girl meets boy, girl loses boy because girl's mother disapproves of boy's menial employment (he is a delivery boy for the local butcher). Boy seeks his widower father's advice. Boy's father goes to see girl's mother and they fall in love. Finally boy's father owns the butcher's shop and boy is learning the trade. The two older people falling in love have nothing to do with the two younger people's problem and is the subplot. In a Regency romance, the lady's maid might fall in love with the gentleman's butler or valet.

Your background experience is used in forming the complicities of the plot and inventing the subplots. Not that your personal experiences can be expected to cover ardent love affairs, being shot at, being left hanging from a cliff, or being thrown into the sea during a raging storm. But you can add to your personal experiences the experiences of friends and relations and newspaper accounts or anything that provides an emotional escapade. Your background of reading is invaluable here, and you will find that some small newspaper item can spark your attention and arouse your emotions. A small item in a newspaper caught Thomas Thompson's attention and sent him off on a research expedition of thousands of miles, eventually resulting in his best-selling *Serpentine*. Although Mr. Thompson was only writing nonfiction at that time, the principle applies to any category of writing, and such an item may well give you the idea for a novel.

Certainly there are far more ideas than books that have been written, which is why I cannot understand the author who is always *about to write* a best-selling novel. This person is usually afraid that if he writes his story, the publisher will steal the idea, or else he just doesn't have time to write it. The path to a writer's success is filled with discarded stories as well as those you wish you had written. The person who worries about some unethical publisher stealing the product of his genius lacks the ability to sit down and put pen to paper. This subconscious defense mechanism effectively stops the writer from beginning something that he is afraid will be unsuccessful. Trite as it may sound, the only way to write a book is to start with the first word and not to stop until it is finished.

Robert Louis Stevenson cultivated the dream state to where he was able to dream complete plots for his books. As a child he was plagued by nightmares, which followed him through to his days as a medical student at Edinburgh. Finally driven to consult a doctor, he was able to control his dreams to where his "little people" were constantly supplying him with plots through the medium of his dreams. *Treasure Island* was a case in point.

For me, another never-failing source of plots is my file of unpublished short stories. The short story market is rapidly dwindling, and I have a file of rejected stories and ones that have never been sent out. These stories, too short to be much more than a situation and unsuitable for extending into novel length, can be combined with another short story and with a little adjustment, one of them can be made into a subplot. Several of my genre novels have originated in my short story file, although I cannot take any credit for the idea. Raymond Chandler's earlier novels were amalgams of several of his short stories that appeared in *The Black Mask*.

It is a very good idea to keep a notebook to record the experiences you hear about, dreams you have, or brief mentions of newspaper stories for plots, themes, or situations. The human memory is far from infallible and it should not be relied upon when you are looking for the right situation to further your plot. And under no circumstances should you discuss your ideas with laymen: Professional writers can be of some help, and it does no harm to bounce ideas off one another, but I would definitely exclude laymen, particularly those who have grandiose ideas for your plots. In my experience, what a layman thinks of as a plot is an incomplete situation that may or may not fit into a plot and always requires a great deal more work to build it up to the point where it can be profitably used.

Laymen always seem to consider themselves experts in some aspect that you have touched upon. Not having written anything publishable themselves, they will take great delight in criticizing your work and even see things that aren't there in the name of friendship. "Why didn't you let me read it before you submitted it?" becomes an all too familiar remark.

Once, because of an illness, my hands didn't work very well and a friend offered to do some typing for me. I was grateful for the offer until I saw the end results. Using the excuse that my handwriting was illegible (which I must admit was true) she rewrote most of my dialogue. My hard-boiled counterespionage agent was talking like a fugitive from a teen-aged romance. I finished up having to throw out two complete chapters and rewriting them.

I really don't know if it is the glamour of the reflected limelight that attracts people like that, or if it is the subconscious defense mechanism I mentioned earlier. It is not worth taking a chance on, so keep all your ideas to yourself. Let nobody but your publisher and your agent see an unfinished manuscript. Everybody else has to wait until it comes out in print.

8.

Outlining

There are two distinct and totally different methods of plotting, and each has its followers. One is to draw the characters so well that with little more than a vague idea of the goal, you can allow the characters to do what is most natural for them, simply follow them, and record their actions and dialogue. The other way is to draw up a detailed outline. I know of a great many writers who follow each method. When I first started writing, I used the first method but dropped it in favor of the second because toward the end, I found that my books would die after a few interesting situations. My advice to new writers is to adopt whichever method appeals most to you. If the first method doesn't work out for you, there is always the second to fall back on. I cannot remember ever having heard of the second method failing, unless the writer lacked the perseverance—in which case it is not the method that failed, but the writer.

By this time, you should have read a whole armful of books in your chosen field. If you have not been able to make up your mind on the several genre books you have read to date, keep going until one particular subgenre stands out above all others as the one most likely to parallel your own style of writing, or matches the background material you can bring to your novel.

Once you have made your decision about the genre, read all the books you have in that subgenre, and read them carefully, analyzing and comparing them. Not that you need to know which page number is the most popular for the first attempt on the protagonist's life, or what size bust is the most popular for the heroine, what you need to know is the possible variations within that subgenre to give yourself a feel for the parameters of the category. The examples I have given in the preceding chapters are simply one or perhaps two in an infinite variety. What you need to do now is to roughly outline the story. By a rough outline, I mean a few sentences that summarize the plot action. As an example:

> A CIA agent is detailed to find the daughter of a highly placed politician who disappeared on a skiing holiday in Switzerland. All the evidence seems to point to a defection, until he orders a polygraph test on all the witnesses. When the results are made known, there is no longer any doubt that she has defected. He is about to put an APB out on the girl with Interpol until the polygraph operator admits that his machine could be beaten by hypnotic auto-suggestion. With this information he sets off to see the key witness. He finds her dead and then an attempt is made on his life. He manages to follow his attacker to a remote cottage where after calling for reinforcements there is a gun battle and the girl is released.

This is the actual outline of the first half of an action/adventure novel I wrote in 1977. You will need to finish the outline, and write similar outlines of perhaps another dozen novels.

Once you have the outline drawn up, go to work on each individual outline and break it down into chapters. Continuing with the same example:

> Chapter 1. The protagonist is having a cozy dinner with his girlfriend when his phone rings with an urgent message for him to report to his office. He has his girlfriend drive him to the airport where he catches a plane to Washington where he meets with his boss and the politician father. With some reluctance, he allows himself to be persuaded to take the case.
>
> Chapter 2. He arrives in Switzerland, introduces himself to the Interpol Inspector who is in charge of the case, and talks to the witnesses. He asks for a polygraph test ot be run on all of them.
>
> Chapter 3. He is introduced to the polygraph operator, goes through the results with the operator and the Inspector and theorizes as to how the machine might be beaten.
>
> Chapter 4. The polygraph operator disappears and the protagonist finds the key witness dead in her apartment. He is attacked by a man who was hiding in the apartment.

That's enough to give you the idea of how it works. For your own novel, this chapter-by-chapter outline can be as simple or as detailed as you like. This is an ideal exercise to enable you to see the structure of a novel. There is no need to go into motivation, either overall or detailed. If your protagonist gets roaring drunk when his girlfriend turns him down, there is no need to mention that he is weak-willed and mentally cannot tolerate rejection, or that for years he has been bordering on alcoholism. All you need is a scene-by-scene summary.

Let's take a look at forming the skeleton plot within the parameters I have outlined for the genre. The purpose of this exercise is to demonstrate the ease with which a basic plot can be formed. I have already given you the basis for a suspense novel with the idea of *The Catnappers* and the Nursery Rhyme Land adventure for a fantasy novel.

Historical Regency romances and science fiction would need more research than I am prepared to give for just an example, and there are too many subgenres in the the mystery field; for this reason I am going to take the (contemporary) romance-suspense and the western.

We will start with the romance-suspense, a simple girl meets boy, girl hates boy, girl finds out that she was wrong, and the book closes with them in each other's arms. To make her hate the boy, we must have a subplot and something to make her change her mind and realize that he is the only one for her. So we'll use two men and make one of them an imposter.

The lead character is an English journalist sent to Nassau to cover an international convention. Never having been in that part of the world before, she gets permission to take a month's vacation at the end of the convention to try to trace her uncle who left England after being accused of a jewel theft. She rents a cottage on the island near Nassau. While she is away from the cottage swimming, a handsome man arrives and makes himself at home, telling her housekeeper that he is her cousin. They spend a quiet evening together and she starts to fall for him. He stays the night but sleeps on the beach. When she looks for him, he is gone and has taken her uncle's last letter through which she had hoped to trace him and prove his innocence in the jewel theft.

She gets a note from her cousin asking her to meet him for lunch at the hotel. When she arrives, it is a stranger who greets her. Apparently the first man was an imposter. She spends a fun-filled day with him and is torn between the attraction she feels for both men. Toward the end of the day they go dancing and he introduces her to a very sophisticated lady who was her uncle's paramour. Too tired to drive back to the cottage, she takes a room at the hotel. Going to her cousin's room during the night, she finds the "paramour" there in a nightdress.

Going from memory, she goes down to the dungeons to find the proof that her uncle was supposed to have secreted there. There she finds the first "cousin" following the instructions in her uncle's letter. They find the papers that Uncle had hidden telling how he had faked the robbery to protect the name of his sister who had used the money to put the protagonist and her brother through college. While they are in the dungeons they are found by the second "cousin" and the paramour who hold them at pistol point, tie them up, and continue to search for the jewels. They get loose and there is a chase through the dungeons that leads to the death of the other two.

Western: The lead character drifts into town and goes into the saloon for a drink. The town bully tries to pick a fight, but the lead is very clumsy and backs down. Before he leaves town he gets the name of the ranch where they are hiring hands, gets a job with the foreman, and is assigned the job of driving the young lady ranch owner to town to the bank. A rival rancher shows up in town with some of his hired hands, and the town bully tries to make a pass in public, but the girl drives him off with a bullwhip. On the way back to the ranch, they are ambushed by the rival's hands who have been instructed to keep them out of the way while her herds are driven off and the brands changed. During the ambush, the lead finally reveals that he is not clumsy, only left-handed, and he saves the girl's life. Arriving back at the ranch they are followed by the town bully. He learns the bully's true name and reveals that he was the man who shot his sheriff brother. Wearing his gun on the left, he picks a gun-fight and then goes off to the rival's ranch just in time to prevent them from branding her steers, He gives the rival owner over to the marshal for rustling.

These two outlines are very rough and need a great deal of polishing before you could begin to use them. I have arbitrarily used Nassau as the location, although I don't know why; I have never been in the Bahamas in my life. It could just as well be set in Jamaica or any of the islands in the Virgin Island group or at any point on the coast of Mexico; perhaps Acapulco, and in lieu of dungeons, you could use caves. One thing that it definitely does need is names for the characters. Reading over what I have written, I find myself getting confused—which would not happen if I named them all.

The protagonist will be Janet Millson, the uncle will be Bernard Peyson, the authentic first cousin is Barney Peyson, the imposter cousin is Michael Craig, and the paramour, Linda Ortega. At this point, I always write these names on a sheet of paper with a list of personality traits, if not a complete character outline, and tack it up on the wall where I can refer to it with a minimum of fuss. I started this habit when I wrote a couple of spy stories and had constant problems remembering how I has spelled the Russian-sounding names.

For the western, the protagonist will be Lou Packett (originally known as Lefty Lou), the girl rancher is Madeline Miles (of the Double M Ranch). The rival rancher is William Spooner, the town bully is 'Gorilla' Grayson, known as Bradley Gray at the time he shot the sheriff.

That doesn't do very much to clarify the outlines, but at least we know whom we are talking about and where the story is going. Before you can start to write the first draft of the novel, you need a complete chapter-by-chapter outline, so let's get on with the next step.

When you have become practiced in the art of writing outlines, it is time to start working on the outline of the novel that you are going to write. Once you decide on the story, make out the first rough summary and follow it up with the detailed outline. In all probability you have some pretty good ideas for some of the detail work, and these should be inserted wherever they fit best. Nothing should be definite at this point: As the novel progresses, in fact, you'll find that you may like to change things around far more than you might have thought originally—one very good reason for writing your outline on 3 x 5″ cards. You may want to have your heroine proposed to, and although you had a romantic dinner with candlelight and wine in mind, the chapter before you have the dinner scheduled they take a walk along the cliffs. From the way the dialogue is going, you realize that it is far more logical for him to propose right then and there. However, her answer will be such a pivotal point in the story you will have to stay with it. If a girl is proposed to, it's no big deal, but whether or not she accepts makes a difference in the outcome of the story. Why she answers yes or no has no place in the outline, unless you are writing a psychological study and her answer is part of an all-encompassing profile of her—although that sounds highly unlikely for a first novel.

Everything has a start, a middle, and an end. I don't know who first said that, and I've lost count of the number of times I have heard it. Once you have chosen your subgenre you will know how the story will end: The killer is going to confess, they get married and live happily ever after, or things get back to a normal schedule. With these finales in mind, the route to each will vary depending on the genre, and there are an infinite number of places to start.

One out of three is a good starting point. What we need now is a central theme. I made enough suggestions in my definition of the genre and the subgenre for you to have a pretty good idea of what the story will be about. So start your outline by introducing the protagonist, possibly the lead character of the opposite sex, and the problem.

Let's assume that you have decided on the main theme and have the rough summary drawn up. Later, I shall be going into much greater detail on the actual start of the novel, but for now let's work on the first chapter of the detailed outline. Before we can introduce the problem, we first have to introduce the protagonist and a little of his/her background. If he or she is a college professor you might like to have them being picked up at the campus by their wife/husband and a brief conversation that will introduce the circumstances into which we will insert the problem. Perhaps they will be talking about a forthcoming trip on their sabbatical to collect pre-Colombian art treasures, or the rigging on the thirty-foot yacht they intend to sail to Suva. Into this conversation comes the basis of the problem: the difficulty of obtaining the right canvas for their sails or the Government regulations concerning the export of art treasures. If you are writing a western, it might be enough for your protagonist to be looking for a job at the ranch, or even just riding into town and getting a haircut and a bath.

Working from the rough outline, you will need to draw up a chapter-by-chapter outline, which may be as complex or as succinct as you like. The main idea here is to get the flow of the narrative. This outline will also be devoid of detail and is intended to make sure that the length of the book is right. Romances and westerns normally run about 50,000 words while suspense, science fiction, occult, mysteries and action/adventure are about 60,000 words. Sixty-thousand words can easily be divided into fifteen 4,000-word chapters, so we are going to make the romance-suspense and the western fourteen chapters, which will make each chapter about 3,500 words.

There is no hard and fast rule about the length of the chapters, and you should cut off every chapter at a natural emotional break. More about that later. Here, then, is the chapter-by-chapter outline for the romance-suspense:

Chapter 1: Introduce Janet, housekeeper, and the basic circumstances: widowed mother who left behind the letter from Uncle Bernard Peyson, who was the dungeon caretaker. Introduce Barney Peyson.

Chapter 2: He gains her confidence with his story of returning home from your choice. They spend a cozy evening and after too much to drink (?) she tells him of the letter. Will not allow him to sleep in the cottage—housekeeper sleeps on the couch.

Chapter 3: The next morning she finds him missing from the beach, returning to the cottage, finds the letter missing.

Chapter 4: Recriminations. Gets the note inviting her to lunch.

Chapter 5: Meets the imposter, Michael Craig, posing as Barney Peyson; is impressed with him.

Chapter 6: Spends the entire day with him. In the evening while dancing he introduces her to Linda Ortega, his uncle's mistress/paramour.

Chapter 7: Too tired to drive home, she takes a room at the hotel. Remembering something she has forgotten (her compact, address book?) goes to Michael's room, sees Linda either nude or in a nightdress.

Chapter 8: Spends the rest of the night telling herself just how rotten men are. Next morning returns to cottage and changes into old clothes.

Chapter 9: She goes to the dungeons and starts trying to search them from memory of Uncle's letter.

Chapter 10: Finds Barney Peyson, who convinces her that he is the real cousin and that he has more at stake than she does, *his father's good name,* and together they continue to search.

Chapter 11: They find a letter that Uncle has hidden from his sister, *Janet's mother,* saying how much she appreciated his action in taking the blame for her theft.

Chapter 12: Michael Craig and Linda arrive with a gun, overpower them, tie them up, and start searching for the jewels they expect to find.

Chapter 13: They get loose and there is a chase that results in the death of Michael.

Chapter 14: Short chapter tying up the loose ends, allowing Linda to escape unharmed and predicting their future together.

As you can see, there is very little detail there and what we have now is a skeleton to make sure that what we have is a *novel,* and not a short story or a novella. What we need to do now is to put a little flesh on the bones, which we will do with as much detail as is needed to fill in the gaps. I have made a few suggestions on the details, but simply to indicate the kinds of details that you might be looking for. The fact that the housekeeper has to sleep on the couch so that Janet has to banish him from the cottage overnight is one such detail that you may want to use. The interior monologue in Chapter Eight where she tells herself just how rotten men are is another (although I would not expect you to use that out courtesy to the sex of the author of your textbook).

Let's get back to the western and see what kind of skeleton plot we can come up with from our rough summary.

Chapter 1: Lou Packett drifts into town, buys a drink at the saloon and asks the bartender where he can get a job. Gorilla Grayson comes into the bar and starts taunting him. Packett fumbles his gun, and backs down from a fight.

Chapter 2: He rides out to the ranch but when the foreman sees how clumsy he is, he gives him a job doing the chores around the ranchhouse *chopping wood for the cook and grooming the owner's saddle horses.*

Chapter 3: One of the cowboys befriends him and Packett pumps him for information about the town and the people.

Chapter 4: He is assigned to drive the owner, *Madeline Miles,* to town to the bank. She takes pity on him and is kind to him.

Chapter 5: William Spooner and some of his hired hands ride in and start painting the town red.

Chapter 6: Gorilla Grayson tries to make a pass at Madeline, and Packett tries to defend her but she drives Grayson off with a bullwhip.

Chapter 7: On the way back to the ranch they are ambushed and chased out into open country while Spooner's men round up the unbranded calves from the Double M. Packett saves Madeline's life and she notices that he is not clumsy, just left-handed *(maybe holding the gun with his right hand and feeding the shells into it with his left.)*

Chapter 8: They are cut off from the ranch and are kept on the run by Spooner's gunmen until he can find a way to outmaneuver them.

Chapter 9: Madeline gets bitten by a rattlesnake and he has to take her into town to the doctor.

Chapter 10: After seeing the doctor he takes her back to the ranch and then rides off to Spooner's ranch just in time to stop them from branding the Double M calves. Grayson is rustling steers for Spooner.

Chapter 11: Back at the Double M Grayson has followed him and he confronts him with the murder of his brother, who was the sheriff.

Chapter 12: Packett puts his gun on the left side and calls on Grayson to fight—You'll never guess who wins! The cowboy who befriended Packett is made town marshal and he rides off with Packett to arrest Spooner for rustling.

Chapter 13: Madeline completely recovers and offers Packett a partnership or the job of foreman.

Chapter 14: Tie up all the loose ends. Your choice: Does Packett marry Madeline or ride off into the sunset?

So there we have two skeleton plots ready to be fleshed out with details. If you compare the rough summaries with the chapter-by-chapter outlines, you will see that there are differences between them. This was done for a reason: to emphasize the fact that the story is not inflexible and will not be until it comes out in print, and it certainly is not inflexible at this point. Had I made the rough summary and the chapter-by-chapter outline match at this point, I would have been committed to the story as I laid it down. Since it is you who are going to write the story, it would be a gross impertinence for me to commit you in such a way.

Go through the rough summaries and the skeleton plots and see what you like about each and what you want to change before we start filling in the details for the working outline. I doubt very much if you will like either of them the way they stand. I certainly don't, but again, this is simply an exercise to demonstrate the ease with which a plot may be formed.

If you are looking to the western, you might not like the idea of my making the lead character self-effacing and would prefer to draw him as a recognized gun fighter who strikes terror into the hearts of all men and with whom all women immediately fall in love. Maybe you want him to be a two-fisted gunslinger, or an impeccably dressed gambler who will spend most of his time at a table in the saloon playing solitaire and waiting for suckers while he bones up on the town gossip. Or you may like to devote two or three chapters to an account of their wanderings out in the open range.

Or if you are looking to the romance-suspense, maybe you are at the point of throwing out all of my suggestions for any or all of the details. You might not know anything about Nassau, or maybe you have a terror of dungeons. Maybe you just divorced your husband because you found him in bed with a girl called Janet Millson and the very metion of the name sends shivers up your spine.

Just pick the parts that you do like and leave them in, and substitute the parts that you don't like with something more suited to your taste, or that you think will have more universal appeal. The skeleton plot is just another stop on the way to the working outline.

Before you can produce a working outline, you need to fill in a great deal of detail that you need to do through research. That brings us to the next chapter.

9.

Research

Webster's Dictionary defines research as, among other things, investigation in some field of knowledge, undertaken to establish facts or principles. In other words, corroboration of credibility. I have talked about using Nassau as the locale for my romance-suspense novel, but before I could sit down and start writing the actual book, I would either have to change the locale to one that I was familiar with or find out a great deal more about the Bahamas.

My shelf of reference books includes an atlas and a complete set of encyclopedias, and the more I try to find out about Nassau, the more convinced I become that Nassau was a poor choice. Frankly, I pulled it off the top of my head because I had heard somewhere that there were dungeons there and that seemed like a most convincing place for a chase with a couple of villains engrossed in seeking out a cache of jewels. My research into Nassau confirms that the historic Fort Charlotte is definitely the site of many dungeons, corridors, and underground stairways, which would make it an ideal place for such a chase, but it falls far short of what I had in mind for the rest of the story. From its location in my atlas I can see that it has a temperate climate, and as such would be an ideal spot for an international congress. But after that the information starts to dry up, and I am left wondering about the difficulties inherent in setting the story of a romance there.

Being far too stubborn to change the locale, my best choice would be to visit Nassau and soak up a little atmosphere. Failing that (and it could very easily fail for financial reasons from where I live), I would seek out somebody who has lived there or at least visited there recently. As a last resort, I would write to the Tourist Bureau of the

Bahama Islands for current information and maps on the island and on the forts containing the dungeons. Only then could I write this story with any degree of plausibility.

From this you can see that there is a very good reason for working authors to travel. I have lived in several countries and frequently use those locales as background for my stories. The only problem with that is the passage of time. I was born in England, but it has been so many years since I was there that any story I tried to write using England as a locale would sound implausible in the extreme. Even the language, or at least the vernacular, has changed; a short story that I wrote found its way into an anthology published by an English house and I was amazed at the difference between the original version and the final printed version.

But there are other means of supporting one's credibility, and a good shelf of reference books is only a start. Apart from personal experience, I would hold other people's experiences and hard-won wisdom at the top of my list. This reminds me of the writer of juvenile stories who was asked if she had any children of her own. "No," she replied, "but I used to be one." Perhaps even more precious than my shelf of reference books is my list of personal contacts: people I have been introduced to, or to whom I have introduced myself through sheer audacity. It is a never-ending source of amazement to me that if I need to know something, all I need do is to write a letter to an acknowledged expert in the field, and if I enclose a self-addressed, stamped envelope (SASE), I am sure to get an answer. I have formed a great many friendships in this way and if one expresses a pronounced interest in their field, most experts are only too willing to share their knowledge with you.

Had I been intending to go ahead with the romance-suspense, once I got the locale settled in my mind, I might have decided to change the jewels for rare postage stamps because Uncle Bernard Peyson would have less trouble concealing them. I know nothing of rare postage stamps—to my mind a rare postage stamp is one you need when you have an important letter to write. So I would go to the nearest philatelic store, introduce myself, and explain that I was writing a book, and would the store-owner kindly recommend a couple of stamps that would approximate the value I needed? Once he is assured I am sincere and not just casing the joint—a business card and a copy of one of my books does the job—he will tell me anything I need to know. I can add his name to my list of contacts, and stop by to see him any time I need further information. Every time I have an appointment with my doctor, I use him for the same purpose. In fact, I think that my doctor would be disappointed if I showed up at his office without a list of questions; he would think I was sick.

I once telephoned Van Cleef and Arpels for a piece of minor information and listened to the assistant manager for half an hour; and for the very first book I wrote (a murder mystery) I made an appointment with the Public Relations Officer of the nearest Police Station and tied him up for a solid hour with my dumb questions. The fact that I was never able to sell that book in no way reflected the accuracy of his answers or the courtesy I was shown (I did sell the next book). Several books later I was able to send him an autographed copy, although by that time I doubt if he remembered my name.

So if it does nothing else, being a writer makes one a very good listener—which seems to me to be at odds with the number of times one is invited to speak at functions. What can I tell them that could possibly be of more interest than what they could tell me? I know a great many writers, and when we all get together, it seems that we do nothing but talk (and drink). It assuredly does no harm to bounce ideas around, looking for reactions. But once we are out of our element, we stop talking and start listening, because that is where the profit lies. I cannot learn anything if I am talking, and I am sure that every writer would agree with me. If I have a choice then, to continue to be a successful writer, I would much rather lose my speech than my hearing.

By getting other people to talk and by listening you will not only become aware of a mass of detail that you would never have been conscious of by reading, but you may get to hear something that sparks your emotions and may serve to act as a theme, a subplot, or even an elusive situation.

One of my most helpful contacts is a lady who works in a travel agency. I stopped there one day to make a plane reservation, and we got to talking. I happened to have my briefcase with me, and when she expressed interest in suspense novels, I gave her a couple of my books. She has profited in that I always have her make my travel arrangements, and I, in turn, use her knowledge to help me with my books. All I have to do is call her up and ask how to get from Mexico City to Anchorage (or wherever my character needs to go), and she will give me the airline, the scheduled times and even what kind of aircraft it will be.

The mere fact that you are writing fiction does not mean that everything you write about should be fictitious. If you start a story where a character climbs into his car in New York and thirty minutes later parks it in Los Angeles, you would toss the book aside—with very good reason. The best fiction is that which is 98% fact and 2% fiction. This is particularly true of science fiction stories: If you introduce something unknown in this time or civilization, everything else must be in accordance with it. As an example, if you have your characters being transported by light beams, you would have no need for automobiles except in a museum.

These kinds of points are subjected to the most critical review, so readers will not only be looking for errors, they will applaud your accuracy. Some of the mistakes that find their way to an editor's desk are appalling. The editor can't be expected to have a grasp on every detail of every work of fiction. That is the author's job, and if you don't know, find out. If, following publication of one of your books, your publisher is inundated with letters of complaint, it will be a long time before he will offer you another contract. But far more important than losing your publisher, these mistakes will cost you your readers, and what is a writer without readers?

Several years ago, one best-selling author (who shall remain nameless) wrote a very good book—except that at one point, his villain was using a .45 revolver. A few pages further on, he removed the magazine from his pistol. That completely destroyed his plausibility for me, and I never could get back to finishing the book. I must admit that I did enjoy the movie, but there is very little similarity between books and the movie scripts based on these same books.

Veracity is one of the most desirable traits that your book can have. Without veracity, you will have no credibility and without credibility, you will have no readers and no publisher. It should be a fairly simple matter to check the truth of any statement you use in a contemporary novel. But to emphasize the same point, if you do not know that the statement is true, don't use it. It's not worth the hassle.

Working on historical romances, Regency romances, and westerns, you'd better be well versed in your subject or you are facing a long haul with the history books. I could sit down and read a historical romance set in Elizabethan England and not know whether the ladies' dresses were described accurately or if these fashions did not become popular until the eighteenth century. But a hell of a lot of people *will* know. Similarly, the protagonist in a western could be using a double action .45 Colt twenty years before the double action mechanism was invented, but neither of these subjects is my forte. All of this is my main reason for staying with contemporary novels in my own writing.

However, there is a bright side to all of this. In-depth research is not always necessary, and there are times when you can fake it. Reverting to the question of using Nassau as a locale—did I mention that I am stubborn? If I write to the Tourist Bureau in the Bahama Islands, I am reasonably sure that I could write convincing scenes in and around Nassau using the maps and tourist information mentioning street names, hotels, and perhaps even the location of the cottage that Janet Millson rented. The thing to be careful of here is that you don't drive the (fictitious) car the wrong way on a one way street, or that you don't have your character drive the car along a canal. I hate driving with wet feet.

The big decision of locale is missing if you are setting your sights on westerns. Since you are a resident of the country of its source, most of your problems will be confined to what it *did* look like a hundred or a hundred and fifty years ago. Fortunately for us, the open land has changed very little since that time. Eliminate the freeways and a few gas stations, scatter a few herds of buffalo around and a couple of bands of redskins, and you have it all ready to come to life. The only thing you might need to take note of is the climate. There is a great difference between Arizona in the summer and Montana in the winter.

Should you be using Montana as the backdrop, you must prepare your characters to be well able to take care of themselves when the temperature dips, and you must be ready to take an axe to the ice that has formed on the water trough. The movie westerns all seem to have been filmed in summertime, and once again there are many more critical readers out there than you might expect, ready to put pen to paper with a letter of complaint to your publisher.

10.

Situations

Once you know that you have a good grasp of the conditions surrounding the story, you are ready to hang the situations on the skeleton plot in much the same way you would hang the shiny ornaments on a Christmas tree. For your romances, each situation must further the development of the feeling on each or both sides while in the romance-suspense and gothic the development of the feelings will parallel the buildup of the suspense.

For suspense novels, each situation must make the final turning point seem even more out of reach, while the protagonist becomes even more frustrated with disappointments. A mad chase across town to find the only person who can supply the answer to the problem will uncover the fact that he has been chasing the wrong person. But the person he *does* find can supply him with a clue to the correct character. A little investigative work brings to light the whereabouts of the right guy—who is in deadly danger—and a race against the clock gets him there just in time.

For your western, let us revert to the chapter-by-chapter outline we have been working on. Each chapter should contain at least one situation to (a) further the romance between Lou and Madeline, (b) step up the suspense generated by the attempted rustling, or (c) make the reader impatient with the length of time it takes Lou to present himself in his true colors.

The occult story brings a gradually escalating series of situations terrorizing the protagonists, a series of events where the terrorizing factor has it all its own way and then a buildup of the revolt against the terror, climaxing with the final showdown where the protagonists emerge triumphant.

The action-adventure story will be tailored to suit the subgenre. The espionage story will have much in common with the suspense story where the lead character will spend most of his time chasing false clues, finding one vital clue in each confrontation that will not be revealed until the final denouement. The straight adventure or war story will be based on an escalating scale of mishaps: Each time, there is nothing left to stop the boat from sinking, no reason for the man-eating tiger to escape the trap set for it, with the Nazis funneling our platoon into an even tighter corner until a stroke of genius accomplishes the mission and clears the way for the D-Day invasion. The man with the mission starts at the bottom of the hierarchy and gradually shoots his way up into succeeding layers of the family until he gets the Godfather.

Science fiction novels will use situations depending on their base story. It may be a story of domestic simplicity with each chapter highlighting a new aspect of technical advances on a strange planet. It might be a story of interplanetary travel, in which case the entire book will consist of situations gradually involving more complex aspects of interplanetary travel, or different planets visited on the way (as per *Star Trek*), or an inboard problem that keeps becoming more complicated until the final climax where the human protagonists are victorious. The fantasy story, as I have outlined it as a possible trip to a mythical nursery rhyme land, would consist of one situation per chapter depicting a different nursery rhyme or fable, e.g., Jack and the Beanstalk, Rumpelstiltskin, the cow that jumped over the moon—and was it Mother Goose who laid the golden egg?

All mysteries, despite the subgenres, have one thing in common: The discovery of a corpse and step-by-step investigation revealing each clue, all of which tells us nothing of the murderer until the last revelation. At that point, one factor from each clue will be put together to point an unerring finger at the guilty party. No matter whether the mystery is a locked-room puzzle, a police procedural, a drawing-room puzzler or a P.I., the mystery writer invariably plays scrupulously fair with his readers and never lets any important clue go unrevealed until the final denouement. The overall plotting is more complicated here than elsewhere. It might make it easier to start the chapter-by-chapter ouline from the back—knowing who your murderer is and writing your plot from the apex of the pyramid down to the base where you decide *who* is to be murdered. With all those clues, you should not be lacking motive. You will, of course, be supplying the standard number of red herrings to put the reader off the track.

You will probably have many incidents already in mind that at some time or other have stirred your emotions and that have just been waiting to come forward to be expanded into situations that will form the substance of a chapter of the book you have in mind. If there is one thing that I am better at than playing "What if?...", it's the game where I have a short conversation with some stranger or intimate acquaintance. Thirty seconds after the conversation has ended, a little light bulb goes on over my head and I mutter to myself, "Now why didn't I say..." Given enough time, I could be a master of repartee, but very few people seem to have enough time to hang around while I'm thinking up a good response. I can always use these smart-ass answers in my dialogue, however; and I'm afraid that I am going to be a great disappointment to anybody who expects to find me a great conversationalist. Most of my dialogue stems from exchanges I have been carrying around in my head, or have taken the trouble to write down. The latest entry in my file is, "I have a cat who is afraid of the dark." Sometimes I have such a good punchline that I tailor the situation to give me an opportunity to use it. At other times, I start a dialogue between two characters, and their conversation gets away from me. If I have drawn these characters so well that they have a personality all their own, it happens far more frequently than I have planned.

If my characters take hold of the dialogue, there is also a chance that they may take the situations into their own hands as well. As I have mentioned before, it might be that your hero has a romantic dinner complete with candlelight and wine to serve as a background for his proposal, but their earlier conversation makes it far more expedient to propose at that time. Emotion, like water, should be allowed to find its own level. The only thing that is important is that you, the author, must not let the story get away from you. Whether she accepts the proposal or not is strictly up to you.

We all have a good situation to start our book. One school of thought is that the author should let his characters dominate the entire book, starting with the initial situation. I know of a great many successful writers who use this method, knowing no more than the final situation, whatever it may be. But unfortunately it is not to be recommended for neophyte writers. If you think this method best for yourself, by all means try it, but if it doesn't work, scrap it and outline your story first. Once you allow your characters free reign with the dialogue and situations, it will not be long before you will have completely lost control of the story. There are many half-completed manuscripts lying around in bottom drawers because the author has written himself into a corner. One of these days, the author tells himself, inspiration will strike and I can get out of the jam and go ahead with the book. The trouble is that it never happens. Once you put a book aside, you put it out of your mind and it is a lot easier to develop another character, put him in an interesting situation, go like hell, and see where *that* one will lead you. Unless you are a polished professional like Marilyn Granbeck, the new one will finish up on top of the last half-finished one in the bottom drawer, and now you will be looking for inspiration to strike you twice. Once you have put aside one half-finished manuscript, your chance of completing another with the same method is zero. Far better to cut your losses and admit that your method is all wrong. This is no reflection on you as a writer.

Later on I will be talking about writer's block and how to overcome it, but there is a great difference between writer's block and a discarded manuscript. Should you feel you know your characters well enough, or *will* know them well enough after a few hundred words of writing that the system will work for you, by all means try it. If you get involved with a permanent writer's block don't feel too bad about discarding the unfinished manuscript. But let it happen twice, and there is something wrong with your system and the only thing you can do is to discard the old system and start outlining. The advantage of outlining the story is that the author knows where the story is going, whereas your characters will never know.

CHARACTERIZATION

11.

Your
People

Once you have outlined the plot, you need a central character to make the story hang together. You can write the book from the first person, from the third, or from the multiple or omniscient point of view. There are advantages and disadvantages to all three.

It is easier and far more natural to record your own emotions in the fantasized situations you put your characters in. Dick Francis, the well-known ex-jockey turned mystery writer, admits to feeling more comfortable writing in the first person. Should you decide on the first person, however, you must temper your descriptions with a touch of modesty. Nothing will lose your reader faster than if you give him the impression that your narrator is off on an ego trip. You may be able to get away with a line like, "his finely-chiseled features drew women like a magnet," in the third or omniscient point of view, but put that in the first person, and you could print your book on hundred dollar bills and still lose the reader's interest.

The disadvantage of the first person POV is that you cannot report any action or dialogue that does not take place in your presence, "The moment my back was turned she slipped the note into her purse." How did you know that if you didn't see it? And you must confine yourself to the *lead* character's emotions. You can tell the readers that you (as the protagonist) were angry, but you cannot say that about anybody else. You can say that the villain stamped his foot, swore, tore his hair, and let them draw their own conclusion. Give your readers all the clues, but let them figure out that the villain acted that way because he was angry.

It is not absolutely necessary to tell the readers everything that occurs in the protagonist's presence, particularly when you want to reveal something at some later time for surprise effect. After all, you don't have to tell readers *every* thought that goes through his head, any more than you tell them when he shaves, brushes his teeth, or goes to the bathroom.

The third person POV follows one person during the course of the story, enabling you to report action and dialogue outside the presence of the lead character, although the entire story revolves around him or her. The main disadvantage of using the third person is that it tends to detach your readers from the emotional motivation, and you cannot report anything that you don't feel deeply. If it is bad for the reader to be confused as to who is doing what and why, it is disastrous for it to happen to the author.

The omniscient or multiple POV has the advantage of clearing up any misconception as to what is happening at any given moment, admittedly more of an advantage for the reader, and it enables the author to write about the emotions of a wide cast of characters outside the lead character's presence.

The disadvantage of the multiple POV is that the protagonist's point of view carries far more weight than does that of an objective observer, thus adding to the credibility of your characterization. "I took an immediate liking to the way she wrinkled up her eyes when she laughed," is more believable than trying to express the same thought from the omniscient aspect—and an essential part of the girl's character shows through. Also, writing from the multiple POV is something like trying to read a play and playing all the parts yourself; it is far too easy to get confused, a fact that your readers will not appreciate. I know of at least one editor who refuses to look at any manuscript containing a change of POV.

Now that you have decided on the point of view from which you are going to narrate the story, you are faced with creating your lead character. There is one infallible rule: You must make him or her capable of seeing the story through to a successful conclusion, but not so capable that it appears easy. Make him sweat a little along the way. Every time your protagonist is faced with a decision, the reader sweats right along with him—and that is what he is paying for.

The writer's aim is to give the reader just enough information to stimulate his imagination, much as the old-time radio dramatizations used to do. Could anybody who heard it forget Orson Welles's dramatization of *War of the Worlds*? You should describe your character's abilities, and let the reader decide for himself what they look like.

The old school that penned lengthy descriptions of people and their clothes is rapidly dying out. It is now considered to be more effective to say, "She was the most beautiful woman I have ever seen," rather than go into raptures over her shoulder length hair the color of corn silk. Everybody has his own taste, and you should let the reader decide for himself whether the most beautiful woman he has ever seen was a blonde, brunette, redhead, or even bald! It is far more important to the reader that she be lovable (or alternately, an absolute bitch) and your first responsibility to your reader is to introduce your characters properly.

Now what gender is your protagonist going to be? Strangely enough, that is the easiest decision that you are likely to make during the entire course of the book. Although genre books are roughly aimed at specific cross sections of the public, there is nothing sexist about this decision, and the sex of the lead character normally reflects the sex of the author—for the simple reason that the male author is more familiar with the masculine emotions as the female author is with the feminine outlook. There have been several cases where the opposite has been true. *Frankenstein*, Mary Shelley's classic horror tale, is an outstanding example with a male protagonist and female author, and *Rosemary's Baby* by male author Ira Levin had a female lead character. There have been numerous cases where the author's sex is in doubt even to themselves, but as a generalization, romances are better written by women for an audience of women, while westerns and action/adventure tales are more successfully written by men for men.

Unless your lead character is the sheriff in a western or a policeman in a contemporary police procedural, he is most likely to be drawn into this situation by mere chance, in which case it will be sheer doggedness and courage that bring him out on top. It is his sense of justice and his inflexible code of ethics that motivate him. He may have found himself in the primary situation through chance or because he has been directed by his superior, but right from the start, you must make it clear to the reader that his sense of values can never be impugned. It is this code of ethics and sense of justice that make your character what he or she is to the reader, and the more the reader likes your hero or heroine, the better they will like you as the supplier of their favorite literature. Looks don't enter into it, any more than they do in real life. Your characters must prove themselves by what they *think*, what they *say*, and what they *do*. It is on this basis that love affairs are built, and the ultimate aim of all authors is to have readers fall in love with their main characters.

It matters not that you spend five or six pages describing the golden tresses, the willow-wand figure, and the deep violet eyes and the long lashes of a character if she doesn't hear her baby cry out for her. It is not how she walks, how she talks, and how she looks; it is what she loves, what she hates, what she fears, what she likes and dislikes, what she dreams about, and what her ambitions are that appeal to your readers.

Your reader must become the alter ego of the characters you create, but the responsibility doesn't rest with the reader, it rests with you as the author. In every case, your hero or heroine must be above suspicion. You are, in effect, manipulating the readers so that they are waiting impatiently for your character to take the initiative to soothe their (the readers') bitter anger at any injustice.

Let the readers become one with the lead character. Your readers should know this person so thoroughly that their ire will be aroused without being told that it has the same effect on your character. Chivalry has been defined as man's instinct to protect a woman from everybody but himself. This is not true in books. Your character must have a rigid code of acceptable behavior and adhere to it without fail.

You can endow your protagonists with vices as long as you don't allow them to interfere with the successful outcome of the story. A great many popular protagonists drink, but they are always there when they are needed and never sleeping off a drunk. Cigarette smoking is rapidly becoming the most unpopular vice in America, and you can allow your main character to be a chain smoker, the type who invariably has ashes spilled down his vest, as long as you don't let it interfere with his performance. In fact, some vices may serve to make your protagonist more human than he might otherwise appear. Just don't go overboard with them. Sherlock Holmes, the pipe-smoking, cocaine-injecting creation of Sir Arthur Conan Doyle, was no less a well-respected figure despite his habits (although I have very serious doubts as to whether Sir Arthur could get away with the cocaine injections in this day and age).

A most valuable trait in any character is a love for animals, and a rapport with dogs or cats will seldom be misplaced. Even though a great many readers dislike cats (more so apparently than dogs), the reader likes his alter ego to be able to overcome this barrier. They like a cat with a thorn in its paw to select your protagonist as a person to turn to instinctively, the same way a kid who has just been robbed of his candy does, or as does the aging whore who has been beaten up by her pimp. If you are considering westerns, it is quite likely that you are thinking about developing such a relationship between the lead character and his horse. Similarly the relationship between the young lady equestrienne and her horse in the romance.

Several fictional characters—notably Raymond Chandler's Philip Marlowe and John D. MacDonald's Travis McGee—are chess enthusiasts. This implies brain power beyond the norm, and the ability to solve complicated problems in human relationships. This is equally useful as a trait for either male or female protagonists who have a complex murder to solve. Without having the actual figures at hand, I suspect that there have been almost as many amateur women detectives as there have been men.

Your protagonist can socialize with the wealthy, realizing that the mere fact that these people are wealthy does not make them happy. Your lead must have an instinctive sense of justice and a perfect record for judging people. He or she is as adept at making friends with the ex-con as with the wealthy, and he or she must be quick to appreciate the injustice when the ex-con is framed.

One of the most sought-after personality traits is a sense of humor. You can fill a dozen pages with description telling how this person has a terrific sense of humor, but you will accomplish more with one humorous line of dialogue.

In *Pale Gray for Guilt*, John D. MacDonald reports the initial meeting between two of his minor characters, Puss Killian and Barni:

> Puss leaned forward and spoke across me, saying, "Gad, it must be the most marvelous, exciting, romantic thing in the world, jetting around to marvelously romantic places! It's really living, I bet. Those fascinating pilot types, and mysterious international travelers and all, I guess you know how jealous of you we earthbound females are, Barni."
>
> There was just the slightest narrowing of Barni's eyes, gone in an instant. She leaned in from her side and said breathlessly, "Oh, yes, it's all my dreams come true, Miss Killian. To fly to all those places in the world," she sighed and shook her pretty head. "But it seems so ... so artificial somehow to use an airplane, don't you think? But with my little broom I can just barely get over the treetops. Have you had better luck?"
>
> "I think having to carry that damned cat makes the difference," said Puss without hesitation. "And wear that stupid hat and the long skirts."
>
> "And it's hard to enjoy the moonlight when you have to keep up that dreary cackling, don't you think?" Barni asked.*

Any comment that these two girls have a sense of humor or for the author to write that they are compatible would be a redundancy, and John D. MacDonald is not in the habit of writing redundancies.

*From *Pale Gray for Guilt* by John D. MacDonld (J. B. Lippincott, 1968). Reprinted by permission of the author and Maxwell P. Wilkinson.

12.

The Traits
They Need

Right does not make might however, and you need to give your main characters sufficient physical and mental powers to make everything come out right by the last page. The talents you endow these people with are to a large extent dependent on the genre and the amount of research you have done. As an example, if you are planning to write an historical romance it might well pay you to make your hero an expert swordsman so that he will be well equipped to defend the heroine's virginity. But swordsmanship would be out of place in a contemporary romance—after reconsideration, so would virginity.

It might be that if you are planning this same historical romance, you might need a degree of horsemanship (they certainly didn't use sports cars in those days). Again, you might be contemplating setting it at sea when they must run the gamut of piracy, in which case you will need to bestow on your hero a certain amount of nautical navigation.

For a Regency romance, you might care to have swordsmanship one of your hero's attributes since this was a "gentleman's" sport in that era, but the best thing to do is to consider the way in which the main problem is to be solved and endow your characters accordingly. The gothic romance is usually, although not always, set in modern times, which will necessitate nothing more than research into the locale. Anything else is superfluous to the main plot: her knowledge of archaeology, antique furniture, or whatever else you have based your story on.

All these physical qualities should be introduced at the same time that you introduce the character, and certainly not as an afterthought. If the reader doesn't already know that Sir Hugh is an expert swordsman, it would be disastrous for him to snatch up a sword to defend Lady Gwendoline's honor; he might grab the pointy end by mistake! His prowess with the sword can be introduced by having him unjustly accused of robbery at swordpoint shortly before he and Lady Gwendoline met or, alternatively, just after. If it is his horsemanship you want to introduce, what better way to meet an eligible man than for a girl's horse to run away. These qualities are all a part of the person's character and must be insinuated into that character's general makeup.

Along with the chapter-by-chapter outline, you should draw up a list of characters and all their personal traits to be used when you insert the situations in the working outline. As an example, for the western:

Lou Packett: Fast left-handed gunman; outdoorsman; expert horseman; adept at all ranch chores; posing as a clumsy, right-handed, semi-ignorant drifter.

Madeline Miles: Young, attractive, inherited the Double M ranch from her father who was killed in a cattle stampede. Hard taskmaster, yet kind; takes benevolent interest in her employees; inspires great loyalty in all her ranch hands.

Gorilla Grayson: Big, strong, fast gunman; bully; drinks to excess; not very smart; always on the lookout for the easy dollar.

William Spooner: On the surface a good citizen; supports the local church; but under it all rustles cattle, and half of his hired hands are gunslingers.

Buck Brenner: Foreman of the Double M; befriends Packett and brings him up to date on all the local gossip; is constantly amazed at Packett's knowledge; eventually is made Town Marshal.

I don't have to remind you that it would be catastrophic to introduce Sir Hugh as an expert swordsman, a magnificent horseman, and a captain of his own merchant vessel. It would be more tactful for him to rescue Lady Gwendoline from a runaway horse and, when she invites him to tea, have her find out that he is a widower with two sons. Then in subsequent conversations with his sons she can find out that he is teaching them swordsmanship while his merchant vessel is in port preparing for his next trip to the South Seas. Of course it doesn't have to be done quite that bluntly; by studying the list of characteristics you have made up for each person, you should be able to see the best way to introduce them. Just don't ever take the reader by surprise, or you may find yourself rewriting three quarters of the book.

If you are planning a suspense novel, many of your protagonist's characteristics will be dictated by plot involvements. Any special talents can be taken from your experience or from research. It is not unusual to find a suspense novel written from the point of view of a woman whose child or children are being threatened, in which case little more than a knowledge of the care of children is required—which eliminates all the crusty old bachelors like myself. Beyond that, the only specialized talents required of the protagonist would be for the background detail. For example, did she meet the extortionist at her job before she got married or at some activity which she doesn't share with her husband? Maybe she is a member of a bridge club that meets while the children are at nursery school. If she is a widow, you will need to mention how she lost her husband, which will need some clarification; it is not sufficient to say that her husband died. (A flashback to the time when he died could easily become one of the most poignant scenes in the whole book.) You must plan the final scene where the villain gets his comeuppance and prepare your protagonist well in advance. It is all very well for your lead character to push the villain out the door of a high flying aircraft and then bring it in to a perfect three point landing, but the first question that will cross the reader's mind is, Where did he learn to fly?

You can depend on the fact that somewhere out there in your millions of readers (You are going to write a best seller, aren't you?) is an expert on some detail that you thought you could get away with. You have only to read the letters to the editor of the Book Review section of your local newspaper to realize just how fast readers pick up on any discrepancy, although in this case they are criticizing the critics who reviewed the book.

During the course of my writing life, I found it necessary to learn a great deal about firearms. Without boring you with all the details, I found that a silencer will not work on a revolver or a rifle and that there is no safety catch on a revolver. Yet my intelligence is being constantly abused by TV shows that show the villain screwing a silencer onto the muzzle of a revolver, and writers who talk of setting the safety catch on a revolver. Set the scenes well to avoid letting your protagonist make a fool of himself, and you.

Even more than romances and suspense stories, the occult genre calls for a normal person in unusual circumstances. It is his courage and code of ethics that will bring him out on top, along with the knowledge that will enable him to beat this evil influence at his own game. Accordingly, more for the benefit of the reader, you may find it more convenient for your protagonist to discover this during the course of the story. Once he realizes what evil he is faced with, he will listen to local legends about this particular force. If it is a general type of ghost or vampire, you might need to do a little research on the matter. Should

70

you be using witchcraft or the Voodoo cult as the villain of the piece, there are any number of books readily available at the public library from which you may care to quote verbatim (with permission, of course). Qualifications of this nature differ from those that we have touched upon before in that they come under the heading of knowledge specifically learned in order to beat the villain at his own game. Swordsmanship and horsemanship mentioned in the historical and Regency romances and the ability to fly an airplane and a familiarity with firearms in contemporary suspense novels are all built-in talents that your characters are equipped with when they first appear on the scene. The main difference here is it is up to you to devise the method by which your character will avail himself of the temporary knowledge.

Action/adventure stories are different from other genres in that they come in two distinct types: one is the unusual person in unusual circumstances (witness most of the series characters, Nick Carter, the Sharpshooter, et al.). This person is *exceptionally* accomplished in all aspects of destroying his enemies, and there are no plot involvements that he is not equipped to deal with. The second type can be classed along with the rest of genre fiction, the normal person in unusual circumstances who must therefore rely on his determination, courage, and ethics. Of the two, the former is the more difficult to write.

It is not so hard to invent a plot twist that would prove to be an insurmountable obstacle to a person like you or me, but when you have a character who is an expert shot, a Karate black belt of the fourth *dan*, an experienced flier of airplanes and helicopters, a speaker proficient in every language, and a man with a photographic memory, it is well nigh impossible to plot yourself into a corner. These are the characters to whom the conclusion of the plot seems too easy. The trick here is not to find plot involvements to extend the lead character, but to find chinks in the armor of this paragon of virtue and to build the plot twists around him.

The normal-person-in-unusual-circumstances covers the kind of story where a mountain climber gets lost in an unfamiliar mountain range or gets lost in the desert when his car breaks down. In cases of this type, you must give your protagonist all the qualifications to survive the danger of his surroundings in addition to bringing the villain to justice—which will all certainly read better and be more educational if you have had some experience in that field yourself but can be dealt with on the basis or research.

If it is your intention to write westerns, you will find that the protagonist is well stereotyped beyond the color of his hat. In addition to his courage and sense of justice, he will need to be fast on the draw and an expert shot, and must have all the talents that enable him to survive in the wilderness. He must be able to light a campfire without a Bic or a paper match, and he must be able to skin for food the rabbits he shoots. The rapport with animals that was mentioned earlier will not be out of place here, and it will not be unusual to find him riding the plains with a dog beside him—a very intelligent dog, naturally. Depending upon the story line, you may want to endow him with a knowledge of Indian tribal customs. But above all, keep in mind the age in which the story takes place: He must be chivalrous to the extreme.

To me, perhaps the most intriguing and educational part of a western is how men survive the wilderness. The protagonist may have to fight for his life with a grizzly bear or get bitten by a rattlesnake, all of which reflects on his qualifications as an outdoorsman. Alternatively, he may be a gambler and never leave the confines of the saloon and dance hall. Once more, the story line and plot involvements will dictate his characteristics.

Your protagonists for science fiction stories will often be scientists with a doctorate in one of the sciences, mainly because the story itself must deal with technological advances based on fact. If you start writing about people from another world invading Earth carrying with them all kinds of gimmicks that would not work on earth, then you are writing pure fantasy. Your lead character need not be a scientist but just a guy who saw a space ship land in his backyard. But for true science fiction, your story should be based on scientific fact not too far into the future. Star Trek is a fine example of true science fiction where all the tricks available to them are based on fact no matter how far into the future they are projected. In any case all the personnel are doctors of some science, and all their calculations and navigations are worked out by computer.

Mystery stories are almost always set in the present and they come in two separate categories: the police procedural and the guy in the wrong place at the wrong time. Although a police procedural makes for good reading, it should not be attempted by anybody who has no knowledge of police procedures. Unfortunately, a great many people feel themselves qualified by the extensive reading they have done on the fictitious subject. This sort of thing should be left to the Joseph Wambaughs. The guy in the wrong place at the wrong time is a far more natural opening for a mystery, as it is with every other kind of story.

The beauty of the mystery story set in modern times is that it does not require any study or research for details, as is required for historical, Regency romance, or westerns. All you need do is to keep your wits about you and write about a locale and a cross section of people familiar to you. Beyond that, all you need do is endow your characters with the talents required of them to overcome the obstacles that the plot involvements enfold them in.

For example, if your setting is New York City, your protagonist does not need to drive. He can take cabs no matter where he needs to go. But if your setting is Los Angeles, the distances are much greater and cabs much scarcer. It would behoove you to supply him with a car and the ability to drive. This brings up the subject of location: For obvious reasons, your story will sound far more authentic if you are writing about a city or town you know well. You might find it more tactful to change the name of certain establishments without changing the location or to refer to them in a general way.

To round out your characters, there is no reason for not using your own tastes in inconsequential matters of personal preference. I seem to remember that James Bond had a taste for scrambled eggs and vodka martinis (though not at the same time), and I suspect that was Ian Fleming's personal taste. If your protagonist goes into a restaurant, why not give your creativity a rest and let him order what your own tastes dictate? Many of my own characters share a liking for crab and lobster simply because it is so much easier to provide them with my own taste than to think up good reasons why they should not like seafood.

You may have them smoke or not as you wish—cigarettes, cigar, or pipe—but since cigarette smoking is rapidly becoming very unpopular, it might be a good idea to have them quit and be suffering the pangs of withdrawal.

You can decide on their preference for liquor the same way you decided on their tastes in food. Unless you are a teetotaler, let your main character's choice reflect your own preference. The reason for this is obvious: If necessary, your protagonist can expound at length on the virtues of your choice of sherry, brandy, or what-have-you or even talk at length on the advantages of teetotalism (perish the thought).

To create a thoroughly rounded character, do not ignore the sexual side. It is the writer's duty to generate maxium reader empathy, and the only way to do that is to draw your character in such a way that he/she has general fascination. Whether you have accepted the current social mores or still think of a simple seduction in terms of a "fate worse than death," you should strive to make your protagonist shine with universal appeal. One's sexual habits are nobody's business but one's own and the proverbial consenting adult. But do not impose your standards on another person, even if that person is just a fictitious character.

I am not advocating that your main character should be promiscuous, but a little sex is good for both your character and your reader. Your personal taste should be the limiting factor as to how far you carry your sex scenes. Any person who voluntarily abstains from sex is something less than human, and we don't want to tag your protagonist with that kind of a label. However, too much creativity in this area will lead you into the field of pornography. Similarly, the restrictions on your language should be a matter of your personal taste.

Once you have generated universal appeal in your protagonist, it really does not matter whether he/she is on the side of the angels as long as they have sufficient reader empathy. In James M. Cain's *The Postman Always Rings Twice* the protagonist has murder on his mind, but Mr. Cain draws him so well that the reader is cheering him on, even though his sole motivation is lusting after the victim's wife (no wonder it was banned in several cities in the thirties!). Another rogue, if not a villain, in more recent times is Lawrence Block's *Bernie Rhodenbarr*, a burglar whose only compulsion is the money he makes from his escapades.

If you draw your main character well and endow him with all the characteristics to make him popular, you will find that you have created sufficient reader empathy so that no matter what you have him do the reader will be rooting for him and you will have added another fan to your list, another person who will buy your next book, and the one after that, and the one after that, and so on *ad infinitum*.

Now that you have decided on the qualities of your main character, you should look at your villains. Much of the empathy that your reader will feel for your protagonist will stem from the despicable actions of your villains. Just as your lead character is prompted by his sense of ethics, courage, and determination, so many of his problems will have originated from the villain's greed or lust.

Not all of your villains will twirl their waxed mustaches or wear black hats in your westerns. Very often the only difference between the good guys and the bad guys is a matter of degree: Quite often you will want your villain to have a great deal in common with the hero. This is particularly true of your romances, where your heroine needs to choose between two handsome, rich young men without being tied to a railroad track in the path of the midnight express. If the revelation of the villain is to come as a surprise you will need to show the reader why your hero or heroine does not suspect him at first. This means that you must write in a sympathetic relationship.

The attributes of your villain will depend on the actual genre. In any of your romances, the final decision will be made between two very eligible men. In any of the action-adventure novels, the villain is a little easier to spot. If you are writing a one-man war against the Mafia, all you need do is give him a Sicilian-sounding name or refer to the Mafia, and your predecessors will have done the rest for you. In espionage books it will do the trick if you simply mention the country and its overall aims of world domination. Russia and Communist China will give you a pretty good start on your villainy, while a World War II story never needs more than an allusion to Nazis, the Gestapo, or the Japanese fighting forces, This is perhaps why stories of POW camps are popular; it is so easy to know who is on which side, except for the traitor.

The straight adventure stories normally have a twist at the end. This means that in the beginning you must draw empathy for all characters in equal portions, unless you are pitting man against nature. Nature always plays fair, and there is nothing malicious about a storm at sea or an avalanche. Mysteries usually contain a surprise in the denouement, which means that you must use plenty of red herrings to put the reader in the right frame of mind to be surprised. A quick run through a couple of Agatha Christie books will make my point here.

Suspense stories may spring a surprise on the reader with the revelation, or they may be written as a chase to catch up with the source of all the villainy. In westerns, avariciousness is the prime motivation of the bad guys, while in the occult there is never any doubt as to the cause of all the mischief. Your reader may not know whether it is a ghost, a vampire, a zombie, or something else that stems from your creativity, but they certainly know that nobody should plan to spend the night alone in that old house.

Science fiction usually draws upon the reader's fear of the unknown to sketch the villains. Here, the reader does not know what to expect on a strange planet (diseases, monsters, or other unknowns). In fantasy, there are good and bad hobgoblins, as well as good and bad elves.

If your story is to contain a surprise ending, perhaps the revelation of the murderer or the traitor, then you will need to develop some kind of rapport between the villain and the reader. The reader already has rapport with the protagonist and you will have to extend this to include the villain. Give your protagonist and your villain an interest in common (besides just broads). They could share an interest in painting, racing cars, or literature; anything you can write about knowledgeably to form a gambit that your characters will develop into a mutual understanding. It is much easier to win when you have an understanding of your opponent.

Give your protagonist respect for your villain, and if it is to be a surprise ending let it be a disappointment to the hero that such a nice guy was not able to resist the temptation that was flaunted. Just the fact that he is playing the part of the villain does not mean that he cannot be personable in every other aspect. He does not always have to sneer or say things slyly. He can smile pleasantly when he says something. One of the main advantages of giving your villain a pleasing personality is that, if you are writing suspense or espionage novels, you can have him or her change sides without giving the whole game away. A woman can go from being a spy to a double agent to being a triple agent, and if she has the right personality, and if the protagonist has fallen for her, you can get away with it.

The only exception to this would be a rotten guy like "Gorilla Grayson", and right from the start everybody must know just how rotten he really is. He is an abject coward and greedy, and the whole tone of the book is to level obstacles in the path of Lou Packett, without the subtleties of compatible relationships. Just as you developed your protagonist, you should develop your villain to do the job that you need doing.

THE
ACTUAL
WRITING

13.

The
Beginning

"A book that I couldn't put down" is an old and well-worn cliché, even if it does make you feel good when you hear it said about one of your own books. What you must avoid is the reader who not only can, but does, put it down, not so much when he gets it home but when he is browsing the bookstores. You've got him hooked if your potential reader glances at the blurb, turns to the first page, then puts his hand into his pocket for his money and goes to the check-out stand.

You have no control over the blurb. Otherwise each and every one of us would be a potential best-selling author. One of my dreams is to be invited by my publisher to write the blurb for my book, and there are a couple of phrases running around in the back of my mind just in case the impossible should happen: "a masterpiece of suspense"—"the love affair of the decade." (After 1990 I will change that to "the love affair of the century.") You do have absolute control of the first page, however, and that will make or break you.

Publishers tend to take short passages from the book, as you have written it, and use these excerpts to emphasize the suspense, the violence, the torrid passion, or whatever it is that they feel they should be pushing, while I feel (quite egotistically) that they should be pushing me. Everybody, including the readers, knows that the blurb is nothing more than the wrapping of the package. Even the most casual of readers will look to the first page to see if his interest is aroused. Otherwise, there would be a dearth of blood-red on book covers: red hearts pierced with arrows or daggers dripping blood.

Every story has a beginning, a middle, and an end, but that does not mean that the story should be told in chronological order. In order to interest the reader, your first page (wherever possible) should set the time, and introduce the main character, the location and, if not present the problem, then at least create the atmosphere for the problem to be inserted. Your first page must also arouse the curiosity of your reader.

A great deal of background material, filling up perhaps the full length of the first chapter, is to be avoided at all cost. If a browser picks up your book and finds that the entire first chapter is devoted to a description of Wigginsville, he is going to replace your book and look for something more interesting. Wigginsville, if there is such a place, may be a fascinating town for those who live there and for historians, but not for the casual reader who is less likely to be interested in Wigginsville than in the characters you are presenting. By the same token, you should avoid the openings that were popular many years ago: "I suppose it all started when I met John Smith," or "This story started the day I met Tom Brown." Such openings are anachronistic, and should you start your novel that way, no reader will get past the first sentence.

The most important chapter is the first in any book of fiction, the most important page is the first, the most important paragraph is the first, and the most important sentence is the first. You will have lost your reader forever, if you cannot grab and hold his attention on the first page. A lost reader can never be reclaimed, which is why you must eliminate all background material from the first page.

If you depend on the reader to stay with you until he gets to the good part, you are fooling yourself. The empathy your reader feels for your main character is what draws him in. Better yet is the promise of action in the first sentence, going on to introduce the lead character, the location, and the time. In romances, action is not necessary because it cannot be appreciated until the reader has grown to know both sides of the romantic liaison.

The action may be appreciated in suspense, western, action/adventure and mystery, and occult stories. It depends on the story itself.

The western story we started to outline could begin in the following way:

> The empty noose swung from the branch of the dead oak tree casting harsh shadows in the noon sun, but the rider scarcely glanced at it as he swung his horse into the main street of Cooper Town. Lou Packett reined to a halt in front of the saloon, tied the black gelding to the hitching rail, and swatted ineffectually at the dust that covered him from the crown of his stetson to his well-worn, high-heeled riding boots.

Here I have introduced the protagonist (Lou Packett), set the place (Cooper Town) and the time (noon). The fact that the lead is dusty implies that he has ridden a long way. The empty noose in the first sentence suggests action to come or just past, although I haven't yet decided which it should be. Perhaps it could be a warning to horse thieves, which would add to the atmosphere. This will arouse the curiosity of the reader enough to keep him reading, and before he can settle down to the rest of the story, he must pay for the book and take it home, which is the whole point of the game.

Consider this example as an impact-bearing first paragraph. It is by an all-time master of suspense.

> They threw me off the haytruck about noon. I had swung on the night before, down at the border, and as soon as I got up there under the canvas, I went to sleep. I needed plenty of that, after three weeks in Tia Juana, and I was still getting it when they pulled off to one side to let the engine cool. Then they saw a foot sticking out and threw me off. I tried some comical stuff, but all I got was a deadpan, so that gag was out. They gave me a cigarette though, and I hiked down the road to find something to eat.*

Recognize that? It's the opening paragraph of *The Postman Always Rings Twice* by James M. Cain, one of my all-time favorite novels. That opener was designed to reach out and grab the reader, and it never lets go until the book is finished.

Mr. Cain brings us into the action with his first line, and the rest of the paragraph is devoted to a thumbnail sketch of his protagonist. It has impact. The reader could no more leave this character than he could make a noise like a porcupine and grow darning needles. You see a fairly shabby character who is down on his luck and your heart goes out to him. No matter how reprehensible he may turn out to be, you will be standing behind him, rooting for him.

This technique is known as the narrative hook, for reasons that are self-explanatory. Today in order to exist, the novelist must hook his reader as soon as possible. Many years ago, the novelists of the Victorian, Edwardian, and Georgian eras had no competition. They could afford to spend an entire chapter filling in the background of a character, perhaps even drawing up a whole family tree. But in this day and age, the novelist has too much competition from movies, TV, even radio.

This technique of the narrative hook is being borrowed by television. By using what they call a teaser, a show displays just enough action, slapstick humor, or emotion to whet the viewer's appetite before

---

*From *The Postman Always Rings Twice* by James M. Cain. Copyright © 1934 by James M. Cain. Reprinted by permission of Alfred A. Knopf.

running the credits. Movies employ the same tactics. Frequently these take the form of a prologue, and I'm not sure that they don't have a good idea at that.

Back to our western. Inside the front cover we could have Lou Packett riding into town to stride into the saloon and back down from a fight with Gorilla Grayson; then at about page four or five, we could run the credits.

Prentice-Hall (in the largest possible type) presents Shoot-Out at Cooper Town by John Stevenson, which would be followed by the copyright numbers, cover illustration by Tom Brown, printing by the ABC Printing Company. That might be exaggerating a little too much. We, the novelists do have the advantage of a prologue when we need to use it, but I'm afraid the idea of using the credits after the narrative hook would not work for us. If you have any doubts, I can assure you that the second greatest pleasure you will have when your first book is published is being asked to autograph a copy. To do this, you must have a place to write your name. And what is your single greatest pleasure? Being recognized on the street.

The romance-suspense novel we have been considering as an object lesson in outlining could start this way:

> Janet Millson swore softly to herself. It was enough to get caught in a torrential downpour in this island paradise of New Providence Island on the way back from the beach, but to find a bicycle sprawled across her path, forcing her to remove her sandals and walk through the sea of mud that had once been the gravel footpath that led to her cottage was just too much. The mailman should have made his delivery and been long gone by now. If she found him in the kitchen gorging himself on Carmelita's cookies and coffee, she would throw him bodily out of the house.
>
> One of the nicest things that had happened to Janet when she had decided to stop over for a vacation after covering the international congress of bookbinders in Nassau for the London Globe was that the cottage she had rented came with a housekeeper who was a cordon bleu chef. Carmelita's prowess in the kitchen had earned a well-justified reputation, and Janet was constantly throwing neighboring gardeners, delivery boys, and mailmen who came from all over the island out of the privacy of her kitchen, so that she could eat in peace.

In two paragraphs I have introduced our lead character, set the time and place and why she is where she is, and am preparing to introduce Carmelita, a woman who will play an important minor part. A role such as this is an asset, as it gives you a means of communicating ideas to the main character, useful should you need a target for your humor. I plan the same thing with Buck Brenner, the ranch foreman in the western. Obviously, the bicycle will belong to Barney Peyson. The introduction of Barney will need more space and give the reader more of an insight into the two characters. At first Janet will be annoyed at his arriving without warning. As the evening wears on, over the excellence of Carmelita's meal, Janet's attitude softens until she is very disappointed to find Barney gone the next morning.

I have already given you a typical example of a narrative hook for a western, and there are two very fine examples of openings for a suspense story with the beginning paragraph of *The Postman Always Rings Twice* earlier in this chapter, and the opening of *Hopscotch* in Chapter IV.

The occult and fantasy stories may lead off quietly: the fantasy, because there is no violence in the story, only relationships between people and hobgoblins, leprechauns, or other-worldly creatures; the occult because we want the appearance of the creature to come as a surprise, and we intend to cash in on the shock value. The opening of the science fiction will vary, depending on the base story. If the story is one of domestic simplicity on another planet, or on earth at some future time, the opening will introduce the characters and their way of life, setting the atmosphere. If on the other hand, the story is one of adventure (perhaps interplanetary travel), you may want to start with action, maybe a narrow escape from a collision with an uncharted comet or an abandoned space ship in outer space.

Action-adventure stories invariably start with violence since, after all, that is what the reader is paying for. It may be necessary to explain the reasons for the violence with a flashback, but the violence will always be there. Mysteries always start off with the discovery of the corpse: Whether you elect to use the murder as your narrative hook or lead up to it gradually is up to you, but you certainly can't have a murder mystery without a murder.

Even if you are not planning any action in your book, it would be well to consider some kind of action to get the story rolling and the reader firmly entrenched on your side. This is true even if it is only a sedentary action, a smile, sitting down, pacing the room: the smile she gives when she sees the flowers he has brought her; the bad mood that the bicycle on the footpath created in Janet Millson; the race against the clock, finishing up with the missed bus; the gun that misfires—he may be on the pistol range. No matter what the action, it will always serve to put the reader on the side of your character, and he cannot become the alter ego of your character too fast.

It might be well to point out that genre fiction can be roughly divided into two separate divisions: the romance and the nonromance. The former has romance as its basic story, with the political events, the suspense, or the romance of the minor characters serving as the subplot. This makes the introduction of the two main characters of paramount importance. With the nonromance, any romance must be treated as a subplot. The characters will gradually get to know each other during the action; their decision to marry, or live together if you are of the modern school of thought, must be secondary to the solution of the main problem.

It might be a good idea to consider this as a hard and fast rule. All romance must start with the introduction of at least one main character; all nonromance must start off with (a) action or (b) creation of atmosphere as a background for the problem.

When you roll the first sheet of paper into your typewriter and start hammering away, there is something else you should think of. Now that you have decided on your opening, ask yourself, Is it happening? Is it going to happen? Has it already happened?

Let us say, for example, that you have decided to open your story with somebody being stabbed. You have three different ways to write this scene: You can focus the reader's attention on the rise and fall of the knife, the screams accompanying it, the distorted facial expressions of the victim and the killer (or should I say the stabbee and the stabber?); you can have the killer fingering the razor-keen edge of the knife immediately before the deed; or you can focus the reader's attention on the blood-stained knife after the event.

In our romance-suspense novel, I used the future tense in introducing Janet Millson immediately prior to her meeting with Barney Peyson. I could have opened with their meeting, but that means that I would have to go back and fill in all the details of both people. This way I have already supplied some of Janet's background material, sketchy as it may be, so that only Barney needs to be introduced to the reader. I am not including Carmelita, since she is only a minor character and has no part in the romance itself. I could also have opened immediately after Janet and Barney's introduction: In this case I would start with Janet's being very annoyed at the unheralded arrival of her cousin and his sweet-talking her into a good mood, not unlike the way I have already planned it.

And what about the western? It could start with the noose having been cut through, a sure sign of a hanging. A sign nailed to the tree might warn horse thieves of the punishment they could expect, or there could be a lynch mob around the jail. There could even be a man hanging from the noose, in which case Lou Packett would cut him down, and if he was not already dead, he would prove to be a very useful minor character, the sort who feeds Lou the kind of information he is seeking, perhaps even being a witness to the ambushing of the sheriff brother. I have avoided Lou's being an actual witness to the lynching because he is too fine a person to stand by and watch a hanging; it would destroy the whole point of the story for him to show his hand this early in the story.

It is extremely important that you get the tense right and stay with it. I cannot recall ever having read a book written in the present tense. I have read a few short stories written that way, but I don't remember having been particularly impressed with them. In addition to my writing, I do a lot of editorial work, and I frequently run across an amateurishly written short story that starts off in the present tense. I say amateurishly written because before the author has reached the end of the second page he is no longer in the present tense but in the past. I know of nothing so confusing to the reader as changes in tense.

The present tense is functional for certain parts of your descriptive narrative as long as it is not allowed to slop over into the action. As an example:

> The smog that *covers* the Los Angeles Basin *is* a dense brown cloud that *hides* the beauty of the mountain ranges from the view of native and tourist alike. Sometimes looking at it Mike Johnson would feel a distinct nostalgia for the clean, crisp air of the Denver of his boyhood. Although he didn't know it, nostalgia *was* quite common in twenty-five-year-old men, and afraid of being accused of being an adolescent with homesickness, he *kept* his mouth shut about it.

You will note that once the descriptive narrative is finished and I am preparing to go into the action scenes, I drop the present tense and adopt the past.

Dialogue as an opener was popular for a while but it rapidly outlived its usefulness. It degenerated into a contest to see which author could devise the most shocking line of dialogue. As such, lines that had no bearing on the rest of the story were being used for their shock value

"Oh, God. Don't kill me."

This has shock value but is of no interest to the reader who doesn't know who is speaking and quite frankly doesn't give a damn. If such an opening is to be used, it must be made relevant by attributing it to the speaker. This line should be preceded by something like this: "She squatted in one corner of the room like a ragdoll with her matchstick-like arms and legs sprawled at odd angles. The only sign of life was in her eyes, which were fixed hypnotically on the gleaming blade suspended over her." This is about as trite as you can get, but it does little to detract from the shock of the line of dialogue. The person does take on a certain substance. We might have an incomplete character sketch, but it certainly becomes less disjointed, and it is a step in the right direction to the main aim: getting the reader interested in the character.

The reader is always looking for character traits with which he can identify—courage, determination, ethics, sheer doggedness. The speaker in this last example has none of these and as such is completely self-effacing. Thus by any accounting this opener would fail disastrously, despite the fact that I have opened with dialogue and action. To put it as bluntly as possible, steer clear of this kind of opening. What you are doing is actually destroying the effects of the rules set down to help you. If you must use such an opening (and I can't see why you should), then do something about the character of the person to give her some interesting qualities. The picture I have drawn here is one of cringing cowardice, something no reader wants to see. Even a token amount of defiance would be more acceptable. Don't get the mistaken idea that if you draw a character as cowardly and self-effacing, the opposite character will appear courageous and determined by contrast. It just doesn't work that way. Should you try it, you are likely to wind up with a book full of repulsive characters that even your best friend would not want to read about.

Just because you have used an opener with action or dialogue is no indication that it will succeed. Temper your openings with moderation and give the reader what he is looking for. Action or dialogue can be used to grab the reader's attention, but only if it involves a character with whom he can empathize. If you need to use a character who has no redeeming features, it's better that you save him for later in the book. There, you can more accurately draw his repugnant character and reserve the opening for personalities with whom your reader can identify.

A narrative hook that pits man against nature is always a safe bet: the sailor fighting the tropical monsoon (or should that be a typhoon? I can never remember which is which, if I ever knew); the skier trapped in the avalanche; the explorer trudging through the sands of the desert under the blazing sun. These are all good openings for one good, solid reason. Your reader will always be on the side of the person and never on the side of nature. Nature, although sometimes very cruel, is never sadistic. Your character may have been exceedingly foolish (who else would walk home from an automobile ride in the middle of the Sahara Desert), but the reader will still be on the character's side because nature does not show any prejudice. Nature provides a challenge to mankind, and the reader is always on the side of the challenger. If he didn't want to challenge nature he should have stayed home; so right there a casual reader can see that he has courage and determination, even if it is misplaced.

One method of starting your novel with an exciting scene to grab the reader's attention is the use of a prologue. It can be based on an event that happens well before the actual story starts. *Shoot-out in Cooper Town,* for instance, could have a prologue that told of the ambush and shooting of Lou Packett's sheriff brother by Gorilla Grayson. It might also be an event that occurs toward the end of the book— Lou buckling on his left-hand holster and goaing out to fight Grayson. Then the rest of the story would be told in flashback style.

Of the two, I prefer the former. A flashback is a very difficult technique to master. The former method uses a more natural storytelling tactic. I think that the opening for our romance-suspense is quite adequate, but if the book should need extra stimulation to bring the reader in, we could write a 5,000 word prologue. In this case we should use Uncle Bernard Peyson hiding something behind a loose rock in the dungeons of Fort Charlotte.

We will not tell the reader what it is that Uncle Bernard is hiding. This way we can have a surprise with the letter proving his innocence when he (the reader) is expecting a cache of jewels. We then can go on with chapter one as planned. The more I write about this book the more enthusiastic I become about it. I am tempted to write it and find another example for this book. To actually write it, however, and to leave it in here as an example might possibly make me prone to a plagiarism suit. Question—can I sue myself for plagiarism?

Switching chapters around is an entirely different technique for providing your story with a good narrative hook. A mystery, suspense, or adventure story told in strict chronological order will most likely have a first chapter of background and a second chapter of token action. The casual browser will not be attracted by all this background material, and even if you put in footnotes that say, "Hang in there, chum, this sonavabitch is going to get his throat slit in the next chapter," it will not do much good. The reader wants to see that you are going to write exciting stuff; otherwise he would be content to buy, or not buy, the book on the promise of the blurb, and we all know what liars the blurb writers are (Prentice-Hall blurb writers excepted).

So if we change our first and second chapters around, we can have the excitement happening first. This proves to the reader that this guy is a rapist, child molester, or homicidal maniac. Then we can cut in with the chapter of background material. With all that excitement behind him, the reader is going to want to know how it all comes about, and he will be curious about what is going to happen next—which is exactly where we want him to be.

It is a mistake, however, to allow too much time to elapse between the two chapters. Switching the two chapters around can only be done when the entire story takes place in a comparatively short space of time. Let too much time go by and you will have created a prologue, and a prologue *is* the background.

Similarly you must not pick for your opener an action scene from somewhere near the middle of the book. To do this, you are admitting that there is no excitement in the book until halfway through. This also compounds the problems of writing most of the book as a flashback and then switching to the recent past.

No good book can be written without considerable planning, and the first chapter needs as much planning as the rest of it, perhaps even more. Give it plenty of thought, and put off your start until you are quite certain of how you will begin.

14.

Dialogue, Narrative, and Transitions

Your novel will consist of two joined parts, the dialogue and the narrative. It is best to maintain an even balance between the two. It is the dialogue that brings your characters to life, and the narrative gives them the reasons for saying what they do and filling in the background setting.

A novel that is overly encumbered with dialogue tends to bore the reader (as many talkative people do by being all talk and not enough action). Too much narrative, however, also drags by being monotonous even when it describes action. Dialogue is easier to read and reflects the characteristics of your people, particularly when interspersed with interior monologues to keep the reader abreast of the reasoning behind the remarks.

I suppose one could write a book without dialogue if your story were of the interplay between animals, much as a book or a play could be written with nothing but dialogue. But to me, two or more people conversing would be too much like psychotherapy. Since our aim is to write publishable novels, we can leave the experimental books for the time that we have had more experience.

The main thing to remember about lifelike dialogue is that it is not natural. That sounds like a contradiciton, so let me explain. We want it to read as though it is natural, but if you were to record a natural conversation between yourself and a friend and then play it back, you would be surprised at just how unnatural it sounds (quite apart from all the "ums" and "ahs"). An actual conversation might go like this:

"Good morning, Joe."
"Hi, Mike. Pretty cold this morning."

"Yeah, not like yesterday."
"I thought for sure it was spring yesterday."
"I'll never get rid of this cold, this way."
"You and my wife both."
"How is she?"
"Apart from the cold, fine."
"And the kids?"
"So far they've avoided colds."
"They must be doing something right."

That is a typical conversation, and if these two guys have something important to say to each other it is going to have to wait until all the social amenities have been concluded. By the time they have gotten around to the purpose of their conversation, half a dozen pages will have gone by, and the reader will be bored stiff. What about giving them a reason for their conversation? Perhaps they are working together, and the point of this scene is where one of them notices the sabotage on whatever it is that they are working on. Then the conversation might go something like this:

"'Morning, Joe."
"Hi, Mike. Did you notice that widget in the corner?"
"The one we finished last night. What's wrong with it?"
"It looks a little lop-sided to me, like maybe one of the legs was too short."
"Couldn't be. I checked those legs myself before we put them on."
"But from here it looks as though it's tilted."
"You're right, it does. How could that happen?"
"I'll be damned if I know. It looks almost as though somebody broke in here and sawed a couple of inches off one of the legs."

This brings the reader into the objective of the scene without wasting any time. After all, the reader doesn't care if Joe's wife has a cold, because if it were an important point it would be dealt with in a separate scene. Nothing that is said between these two men is of any importance except the fact that the widget has been sabotaged.

Another thing that you may have noticed about the preceding dialogues is that I have completely dispensed with the "Joe said," "Mike said." A great many fledgling writers feel that they have to identify every line and, with a horror of repeating themselves, overwork such verbs as ask, inquire, query, demand, reply, respond, retort, and answer. These kinds of verbs used continuously will make your characters sound pompous. Had this been a three way conversation, I would have had to identify the speakers, but I could have done that quite simply by using said or asked. As it is, a two way conversation can stand on its own once we have identified the speakers. In the majority of cases, the remark itself will identify the speaker.

"I think I first fell in love with you when I saw you walking toward me in the garden in that yellow dress with the sunlight in your hair."

You don't need to be told who is saying that unless one of your characters is in the habit of wearing drag. And if he is, what kind of a book are you writing?

Or you might write a paragraph about a guy driving his car into his driveway, getting out, locking the car, walking up the path to the house and letting himself in.

"I'm home. Have we got any gin? I'm bushed."

"You're late again. If you wanted a martini you should have bought some gin on the way home."

"You're supposed to take care of the house. Can't you do anything right?"

That's the start of a good old-fashioned knock'em down drag'em out fight, and it still isn't necessary to identify the speakers with Tom said, Jane replied. There is a very definite purpose in that dialogue. We are not just passing social amenities between these two people, they are on the point of having a fight. Should we be using this, I would expect the conversation to end in a separation, maybe a divorce, or even an attempted murder—nobody likes a person who runs out of gin. This, then, is the object of the scene that will advance the plot or give the reader some additional information, such as the crippled widget in the previous dialogue.

Although dialogue reads fast and easily, a long unbroken paragraph of dialogue is just as monotonous to the reader as is a long unbroken paragraph of descriptive narrative. If you are bringing your lead character into a setting for the first time, instead of using a complete paragraph to describe the room and then go on to recount the conversation, mix the two up. Start the dialogue and intersperse a few descriptive phrases to give the reader more of a feel for the setting.

> When Lee pushed the buzzer it was the Senator's wife who answered.
>
> "Mrs. Swain? The Senator is expecting me."
>
> "Mr. Holt, he had to go out for a few minutes, but I told him that I would entertain you until he got back. Come in."
>
> She turned and led the way from the entrance hall through the den which was furnished with a massive antique desk,

oak paneling and a collection of swords and knives, among which were a Gurkha *kukri* and a Malay *kris*. Lee followed the gently undulating hips through the sliding glass doors out on to the patio. All good things have to come to an end and it was behind the bar that the metronomic lilt of the hips finally stopped their provocative swaying and Lee could turn his attention elsewhere.

"Drink?"

"Whatever you're having."

The senator's wife was very tall and it was a long way down to the bar shelf, which gave her an opportunity to show Lee that there was something more than flowers to look at on the patio. She waved her hand at a rustic chair under an umbrella but he ignored that, and walked across to the railing where he could look down at the Pacific Ocean.

Mrs. Swain was reluctant to give up her pose but finally straightened up and brought him a hefty shot of bourbon that barely covered the solitary ice cube. She touched glasses with him, perched one well rounded hip on the railing, and looked at him expectantly.

"Did the Senator say what he wanted to see me about?" He sipped the bourbon tentatively. It must be 90 proof at least.

"My husband and I still have a few secrets from each other." She leaned back and gave him the full treatment. The full treatment was lining herself up with the setting sun so that it shone through her hair giving her a halo effect, a movement she must have practiced over and over until she knew exactly where to perch on the railing for which guest. Lee felt like applauding but thought that would be in poor taste.

The above description contains a mere six lines of dialogue, but I have managed to get in a description of the senator's wife, her sexy ways, and a description of the den and the patio. This makes for easy reading without losing any of the atmosphere.

Condensed action can also be very useful. The preceding scene is necessary to give the reader information he would otherwise not have, and all the points I have mentioned can be used further on in the story. It is fairly obvious that the Senator's wife would not reject any advance and might instigate a seduction herself. The den with its massive antique desk where something may be hidden: or one of the daggers on the wall might be used in later scenes. If you are going to use something you must first place it, and for heaven's sake don't say, "He snatched a Malayan *kris* from the wall and stabbed him," unless the reader already knows that there is such a weapon on the wall.

Condensed action is where you get your character from one point in the story to another without bothering the reader with all the finer details:

> Since we had plenty of time at our disposal we elected to fly to Australia the long way, changing planes at London, Teheran, and Hong Kong.

This is a technique, however, that can be easily overdone:

> It would have been faster to fly directly to Australia, but since Lydia had never seen the birthplace of her mother in Teheran and I still had an uncle in Hong Kong who might be able to give me some contacts in the Far Eastern market, we decided to break our journey at Teheran and Hong Kong. But while we were in London, riots broke out in Teheran and I heard from my mother that my uncle had died, so we flew straight through from London.

Obviously there is a great deal missing from that passage, not the least of which is the motivation of the characters. Consequently it reads more like a fifth grader's composition, "What I did last summer." If one of your characters has motivation, it is worth writing fully. If there is no motivation beyond the destination and a change of locale for the next scene, it can simply be used as a transition.

Condensed action is used in transitions to prevent the readers' being bored with passages such as this:

> There was nothing more that could be done before morning so I dropped Lydia off at her apartment with a promise to pick her up at eight-thirty for breakfast. I took the freeway to King's Street and was able to find a parking spot in front of my apartment. I picked up my mail, went inside, poured myself a shot of bourbon, and settled down to read my mail. Most of it was junk mail, but there was one personal letter from my Aunt Agnes. I knew that if I put it off I would never answer it, so I got out the typewriter and sent off a quick note telling her what marvelous weather we have in Southern California while the rest of the country is snow-bound.
>
> By that time it was eleven o'clock and I got undressed, set the alarm for seven, and climbed into bed. I slept well and dreamlessly and awoke refreshed and even sang in the shower while the coffee was percolating. I brushed my teeth, poured a cup of coffee and took it into the bathroom with me while I shaved, then dressed in my fawn slacks, white shirt, striped tie, and tweed jacket and loafers. I put Aunt Agnes' letter in the mail, climbed into my car, drove to Ernie's service station, and had them fill the tank and check the oil and water, drove over to Lydia's apartment, and took her to breakfast.
>
> Over pancakes and sausages and coffee I said, "I'm really not convinced that Mr. Robinson was telling us the truth yesterday..."

That should be enough to put any reader to sleep and you will bore every reader before the story picks up again. There is absolutely nothing there that is relevant to the story line, and about the only thing I have omitted is any trip he made to the bathroom. Such a passage should be written this way:

> There was nothing more that could be done before morning, so I dropped Lydia off at her apartment with a promise to pick her up for breakfast at eight-thirty.
>
> Over pancakes, sausages, and coffee the next morning I said, "I'm really not convinced that Mr. Robinson was telling us the truth yesterday..."

Here I have dropped the story at the end of one scene and picked it up at the start of the next scene, much as in a play or movie. The only omitted material is the irrelevant coincidental action. We can safely assume that a man shaves every morning, brushes his teeth, and goes to the bathroom at fairly regular intervals. As we assume this, our reader will also assume it. Anything you might want to include must have a purpose. If you tell the reader that he shaves, it might be that he had been intending to grow a beard and for some reason changed his mind. Tell the reader that he went to the bathroom and you must have a story-related reason: For instance, he has been constipated and just tried a new medication, although what the hell that has to do with the story I shall never know, nor do I want to. After all, this is a novel, and we can dispense with the commercials that plague us on television.

We can consider the use of dialogue to bring information to develop the plot, the use of narrative to describe the settings and action, and the transitions as means to change the action from one scene to the next, although they are not strictly limited to these functions.

Dialogue can emphasize character traits, in effect taking some of the load from the narrative and putting it on the dialogue; but as I said before, dialogue is easier to read than narrative, particularly when it comes to accomplishments. If a character's politics need to be accentuated, a line like, "Yes, we met at the last Democratic convention," will do the job without tagging the loyal Democrat label on to the descriptive narrative.

However, a character's political preference will be of no consequence in the usual story unless he is an anarchist. I'm not at all sure that anarchy is considered to be a legitimate political party; they don't have an established headquarters, I'm quite certain. On the other hand, a Nazi is a member of a political party, and the Nazi label automatically labels the guy a villain.

Many of a character's personal traits can be included in brief action sequences by implication, rather than being encompassed in the descriptive passages. If our man drives a souped-up '57 Chevy, he is a car buff, and if the scene has him coming out of a karate gymnasium, that takes care of another characteristic. Of course, you can always have him coming out of a pool hall and boarding a local bus. It all depends on what you have in store for him later on in the story. If he comes out of the karate gymnasium and climbs into his '57 Chevy, you are prepared to involve him in a car chase and in hand-to-hand combat. If he leaves the pool hall and boards a bus, it would sound artifical if he turns out to be good driver and a karate expert. Above all else, your book must sound logical.

Once you get started on the writing, don't try to emulate any particular style. Your style will come naturally as you express your thoughts; style is the product of a natural growth. As you continue to write, your style will become obvious, and you will be the first person to realize it. Your editors will recognize your style as you become published, and one of the most encouraging forms of rejection notice is the one that says, "I like your style, but we are overloaded with this kind of story. I'd like to see something else from you." This is the kind of thing that editors do from time to time, and it proves that editors are not all as stone-hearted as we have been led to believe.

Use humor, metaphor, and simile in your writing, but don't let them sound strained. I use humor in my writing just as it occurs to me in the writing of the first draft, but if you use a metaphor or a simile just as it occurs to you, it is liable to sound trite. A metaphor must always sound natural and smooth but sometimes it may take hours to find the right metaphor or simile to read evenly, as though it were all a part of the natural flow. If you get to a place in your writing where you feel a metaphor or simile is called for, use some trite phrase to keep up the flow, then later look for an original expression to replace the "white as a sheet" or whatever you wrote down as you went through the first draft.

Metaphors and similes are invaluable in describing the physical attributes of your characters; they leave a lasting impression on your reader. If you say that a character has a big mouth with large unevenly spaced teeth, it would make little or no impression on the reader; but if you should say that he has a mouth like a graveyard, the reader will get a visual impression of him every time he speaks.

Don't try to write regional accents into your dialogue; it is far better to name the accent. Call it a Southern drawl, a midwestern accent or a Bostonian inflection, and let the reader's imagination do the rest. Most readers know what an English accent sounds like, and if you spell "very" as "veddy" it looks not only foolish, but it is difficult to read. Despite the fact that I was born in England myself, I have yet to meet an Englishman who says, "pip pip." If necessary, you can use solecisms to emphasize the accent: Phrases like "I seen him," "I brung me dawg," or

"Y'all come back" are fine, and will make your point without your having to rewrite the entire language or adopt a phonetic alphabet.

Another point to bear in mind with dialogue is that unlike the spoken word it is written so there is no emphasis on any particular word. A very brief example of this is contained in the sentence, "Did he do that?" Looking at that, any of those words could be stressed changing the whole meaning of the sentence. "Did *he* do that?" is quite different from "Did he *do* that?" You could italicize the word to be emphasized by underlining (if your typewriter is not equipped with italic type), but if you are careful structuring the situation, the context itself should indicate which word should be stressed.

Transitions can be used to indicate change in time or location. The time transition is the one that is used for a flashback. Perhaps the most successful of these is the prologue, where literally no transition as such is needed. The prologue starts the story off with Uncle Bernard Peyson hiding something in the dungeons in our romance-suspense, and then there is a break and chapter one finds Janet walking up the beach to find Barney Peyson in her cottage. In our western "Shoot-out at Cooper Town," the prologue starts off with the ambush and the murder of the sheriff brother, and then chapter one goes straight into the arrival of Lou Packett in Cooper Town.

There is a system of dating every chapter, but I cannot see much advantage in doing that unless the basic story is a race against time. A man is perhaps scheduled to die in the electric chair at 6A.M.on Friday the 13th, and the story opens with the protagonist starting his investigation on Monday the 9th. Any time I have ever read a story like that, however, I get the impression that the characters are doing far more than they have time for. Consequently, the story seems somewhat forced. The only other time I could see any advantage to dating is where there is a great deal of time elapse between chapters, as if you were following the fortunes of one particular family from the times of, perhaps, Henry VIII to the present. In this case, of course, you are going beyond the realms of genre fiction and are getting into family sagas. I could perhaps recommend that technique when there is a large interval of time between the prologue and the first chapter: for example, a skirmish in the trenches in France in World War I, with chapter one starting with the routing of the British Army at Dunkirk in World War II.

15.

The
Length
of the Book

You will know well before you write your opening paragraph just how long your novel will be. There are fairly standard lengths for novels in each subgenre, and the length is almost as much a part as is the structure of the plot involvement. From this you can schedule your daily workload, a schedule that must be rigidly adhered to once you have decided upon it.

By experimentation you will easily find the amount of writing that you can accomplish in any day. Multiply that by five, six, or seven, depending on the expected length of your work week, and from there you can predict the dates of the conclusion of each chapter and the date of the end of the novel itself. Do not set yourself too difficult a task or you will find yourself substituting quantity for quality. It is better to plan a minimum word count, one that you must reach, and a maximum count with which you can reward yourself if you reach it, perhaps by giving yourself an extra donut, or permission to watch a late night movie on TV. Whether you write in the morning or in the evening is a matter of personal preference, must be arranged to fit into your working schedule, and depends on whether you are a 'morning' person or a 'night' person.

An idiosyncrasy that I have picked up over the years is to carry a running total of my words on my calender so that at any time, I can tell my agent that I am halfway through, twenty percent complete, or whatever it may be. (At the start of this chapter I was 70% complete.) A similar method will prevent you from finishing a novel that is ridiculously short on word count, or just as ridiculously long. When a publishing company stipulates the word count on their writer's guides, they expect you to observe them within certain parameters. If they ask for a 50,000-word novel, they will not be satisfied with 35,000 words or 65,000 words. You can probably get away with 45,000 or 55,000 as long as the variation in length is not reflected in the story line. If the last chapter is rushed and the count stands at 55,000 words, something is wrong with the body of the story, and something should be taken out of it. Let's talk more about that in the next chapter.

By scheduling your work load you will bring order into what otherwise may be chaos. Of all the professional writers I know, all but one work to a set schedule of words or hours per day. The one exception is Michael Shaara, the Pulitzer Prize winning author of *The Killer Angels,* who admits to writing only on inspiration and never to a stipulated number of words or hours per day. I can see how that might work for his short stories, but it is difficult to imagine how it would work for a major novel of such importance, one that would be considered for an award of such consequence. Most writers do pen their short stories as and when they get the inspiration with a fresh idea, but a novel would be no more than a vague outline of theme.

A theme can always be executed into short-story-length on inspiration. A novel-length book would need fresh inspiration with each succeeding situation. I am not saying it cannot be done, however, and should you feel that this method is your metier by all means try it. If it is unsuccessful you can always write your second book with a little more planning. Whether you work for a stipulated number of hours a day, or write to a minimum/maximum number of words per day is up to you, as long as you write your set apportionment on a regular basis. On the pain of never finishing a book you have started, don't start and then pause until you feel the mood before you continue. You may be quite successful in writing just whenever the mood suits you, but according to the law of averages you would spend at least as much time in idleness waiting for the mood to strike you as you would at work. You may take inspiration from Dennis Lynds who writes mysteries under the name of Michael Collins. Dennis's work has been compared to Ross MacDonald's Lew Archer series. He writes seven days a week, fifty-two weeks a year, and goes on for years without taking a day off. If he were to wait until he felt in the mood he would have halved his prolific output. Most writers don't like the actual process of putting words on paper, and it is far too easy to find excuses for not writing. There is always something to read, letters to write, phone calls to make, anything to use as an excuse for not writing.

Ernest Hemingway always stopped his day's work in the middle of a sentence, because he found it so much easier to start again the following day. Perhaps you have a wife or husband who will call you to supper at the crucial point of each situation, in which case you might find it easier to emulate Hemingway's method. I still seem to be able to finish every book I start however, without resorting to any such drastic measure as getting married.

You may find it difficult to start your day's work if you have stopped the day before at the end of a chapter, a situation, or an action sequence. When that happens you need to go back and read the last dozen or so pages to get the feel of your characters and the urgency of the situation, which is why so many writers (myself included) always start their day's work by reading a minimum of the previous day's output. Even with a textbook such as this I feel the need to do so, but part of the reason for that is the fear I have that I will either contradict or repeat myself.

Once you have your detailed outline, you should be ready to take the story from the opening paragraph through to the resolution of the final climax. Your story should not be inflexible at this point: Much will depend on the way your characters develop. Characters have a way of developing themselves, and sometimes they tend to take the story off at a tangent. You should write your detailed outline on two sets of 3 x 5 cards: one that follows the main plot, and one that outlines the subplot and situations. The advantage of this is that the second set will lend itself to being reshuffled without interfering with the continuity of the story line. In this way you will be free to add to or subtract from the situations as they occur to you. What may seem like a good idea for chapter two can turn out to be in conflict with the character's personality at that time and may be better reported in chapter fifteen when that particular facet of his or her character has been more fully developed.

This is particularly useful in writing action/adventure novels where there is some kind of a fight in every chapter, with very little difference made between the methods of fighting (except for the antagonists). The same thing can be done with other subgenres: changing your locales around, love scenes between minor characters, and the chance to use your sense of humor.

Somewhere between your opening paragraph and the resolution of the final climax you are likely to run into the nemesis of all writers, writer's block. Writer's block happens to all of us, some more often than others, and the only way to deal with it is by hard work. If you are working from a detailed outline it might take the form of a complete blank where you are unable to put two words together to make sense. If you are using a system of allowing your characters to guide you in the formation of the plot, writer's block will be the total inability to know what is going to happen next. The book will never get finished if you sit back and wait patiently for inspiration to strike. The only thing to do is to keep writing. Inspiration never comes to fill an empty head. By catering to this feeling of writer's block you are losing all the momentum you have built up. This makes it difficult, if not impossible, to replenish. If you keep on writing, you will find that what you thought of as writer's block has evaporated into thin air. Even if you have to throw out several pages you will discover that the next situation will form itself on the paper as you are writing. Try taking a break from the story line. By this time, and writer's block never happens in the first chapter, you will know your characters well enough to take them away from the scene and put them in an entirely different setting, even a different era, and write a completely irrelevant scene using the same characters. Let them go out to dinner, or go to buy a car, or better yet, write a dialogue or philosophize on the relative merits of several different cars. Keep on writing, and somewhere along the way one of the characters will suggest a line of dialogue or action and almost without knowing it you will find that inspiration has struck again.

Not to be confused with writer's block is the habit so common to most fiction writers of writing themselves into a corner. You make a good, interesting start, you build up your characters and everything is going along according to plan, and somewhere around halfway through you suddenly find that you don't know where you are going. You know that eventually everything will come out as planned, but suddenly the sequence of events seems unreasonable, maybe even the situation you are currently involved with seems unreal and illogical.

The problem is not the current situation even though it may appear to be, for it lies deeper and further back than that, and the only way to cure it is to go back through what you have already written. Somewhere along the line, usually about a dozen pages earlier, something has happened. Something that somebody said or did launched an action or a dialogue that, since it appeared to be a diversification with great potential, you followed. It might not be as simple as that. It might be a revelation of a single facet of a character's personality or a line of dialogue that just slipped out unplanned. but whatever it is, it is the core of your present dilemma. If you rewrite that page, you will find that the situation and those following it will change sufficiently for you to get past the offending passage.

Writing oneself into a corner is quite common and there is a tale, almost a legend by this time, of one of the earlier writers who made a living before the advent of the pulps by writing serials for magazines. The first time I heard the story it was supposed to have happened to Arthur Conan Doyle, but I have since heard it attributed to several other leading writers of that time. This writer sold a serial story of men's adventure to a leading magazine and every week, right on time, he would deliver the next week's episode. He was a good writer and was not only able to instill a sense of urgency in his readers, but also among the editorial staff at the magazine, and in truth he must have had the largest following of any writer. Every episode would surpass the last in excitement, and his protagonist weekly got into more trouble than anyone would have thought possible.

Week after week each episode brought more danger to this long-suffering character. Then, while the country paused with baited breath until the next issue came out with the solution, he would come up with an even more desperate situation. Finally the villains threw the hero into a well with steep sides that afforded no hand or footholds. There were no ladders or ropes, nothing that might be used to climb out. The whole country held its collective breath wondering how their hero would resolve this latest setback, none more anxious than the editorial staff of the magazine. The day of the deadline came. Everybody waited expectantly for the appearance of the writer with the next episode.

Minutes dragged into hours. Five minutes before closing time the writer arrived with the neatly typed episode and handed it into his editor. The editor (who was perhaps the most anxious of anybody) slid it out of the envelope and the first words that met his eyes were, "When I was finally able to get out of the well."

The story does not go on to tell of the suffering that the writer was subjected to in his frustrating search for a solution to the problem. Had he been writing a novel he could have reread the last few episodes and perhaps rewritten them to give himself a way out, but since the entire thing was in print up to that point, he needed to produce the answer immediately and had no choice. You, as a writer of novels, have every opportunity to study the situation and perhaps rewrite parts to give yourself a way out. Almost invariably you will find that the answer to your problem lies about a dozen pages earlier, but don't for heaven's sake, say, "Once he had resolved the problem," or "found the answer."

You are sure to have read countless books in which, by the time the protagonist gets deeply involved in the problem, you are asking yourself how anybody could be so dumb. You wonder why he hasn't questioned the facts that present themselves, thus avoiding the problem altogether. The answer is simple. If he were too smart to get involved in this problem there would not be any book. Here is a point that you should bear in mind: If your character is too smart, there ain't gonna be any book. If Janet Millson had seen through her bogus cousin and fallen in love with Barney Peyson in the first chapter, you would have had a short story rather than a novel.

Had Lou Packett worn his gun on the left side and admitted to being a fast gun, he would never have found out who ambushed his sheriff brother, and even worse, he would never have met Madeline Miles.

You need these details to build up the problem, but just make sure you don't oversimplify them. You must get maximum reader empathy for your characters, and your reader cannot empathize with anybody who is stupid. If you ever try to read a book with a dumb protagonist, you will never get through the book. Even children's books have smart characters. My six-year-old neighbor has a collection of "Bugs Bunny" and "Mickey Mouse" books, and I'm not at all certain that they are not smarter than many of the characters I try to create. And if you are wondering why I don't discuss children's books, juvenile literature is not included in genre fiction, and deserves a separate study.

Mention has been made of flashbacks and the way they can be used to fill in background material. When starting your novel off with action, a flashback is almost imperative to show the reader just how the situation came about. But beware of overusing this valuable tool.

Constant flashbacks to draw a character's background can be disastrous. The trouble with a flashback is that it stops the action. When you transport the character back in time where some little point reminds her of some happier time, you put the brakes on your plot. The point to remember in your story, any story, is that the action must supersede all else, and anything that stops the action should be thrown out.

Flashbacks can be used in the same way that we used the descriptive narrative, interspersing it with action rather than dialogue in order to keep up the pace. Remember, the only reason you are using a flashback is to avoid the long, monotonous passages that trace a person's life back to the time of his or her birth. Such points can be made very easily without interrupting the flow with brief comments. Such as:

> He walked over to his car, parked in front of the florist where he had first met Glenda.

Not enough detail? Maybe so, but isn't that better than:

> He walked over to his car. Climbing in he noticed that he had subconsciously parked it outside the florist where he had first met Glenda and his mind went back to that day when he had slipped into the store to avoid the torrential downpour. He was browsing among the flowers trying not to look self-conscious when she had approached him. "I need a corsage," he said quickly to take the initiative.
> "Do you have anything special in mind?"
> "It's for a beautiful girl with the same coloring as yours."
> She had picked up an orchid and held it on her dress. "How about this? It must be a very special occasion."
> "It is," he had said. "Our first dinner date."
> "Shall we deliver it? I'll need the name and address."

"What *is* your name? We can leave it here." She had been offended at first, but had reluctantly agreed to go to dinner with him, and they had often laughed about the way he had tried to avoid a thunderstorm and wound up with a wife and three kids.

All this is doing is replacing that monotonous passage of background with a batch of irrelevant material that detaches the reader from the action. The only relevant part of that passage is that he got into his car, apparently to drive somewhere so that the next scene can take place.

If the way they met or the orchid has any significance, it should be treated separately and not included in such a way as to stop the action. Now that so many writers are using word processing in lieu of old-fashioned typewriters, somebody should devise a program that would automatically delete phrases like, "Her mind went back to the day..." "She recalled the time she had first seen him..." or "He remembered the day on the lake..." Anybody who can invent such a software program will make an instant fortune among fiction writers.

When long flashbacks are necessary to give the reader more detail, then the problem lies with your time span. If your story covers a time span of just a few days while a married couple are settling their differences, there is no need to mention the day they met. On the other hand, if their original meeting is of significance, your time span should be increased to start at the time they met and follow them through their courtship up until their present differences of opinion. It should be quite obvious to you that such a brief flashback will not obstruct the action, and the fact that the man is a sentimentalist is a necessary part of the story, a part that could almost be done with an adjective or adverb.

Perhaps you are considering a phrase such as: "Mark was a big, sentimental slob..." Here the brief flashback is preferable, because it shows rather than tells.

Ever since he had first met Glenda in the florist shop, Mark had given her a yellow rose on every birthday, a red rose on their wedding anniversary, and an orchid on the anniversary of their meeting.

A rule to remember is that visualization is always better than telling. After all, what does a sentimental man look like? We all know what he does, but what does he look like?

In chapter one we discussed writing techniques, and a great many professional writers, certainly the most prolific ones, use a single draft with just a light review as it leaves the typewriter. Some of the biggest names in the literary world (for example, Sidney Sheldon and Colleen McCullough) use countless drafts on the way to the final presentation. You will be looking at reviewing, revising, and rewriting in the next chapter, but must not put all your faith in what you can do with your revising.

There is a perfectly natural tendency to tell yourself that since you are going to go back to review and rewrite the entire manuscript, you can settle for something less than your best work. Unfortunately, such an attitude will only escalate into sloppy workmanship. Before you know it the first draft of your manuscript will become no more than a series of shorthand notes. Such brevity and succinct phrases were ideal when you made up your first outline, leaving your metaphors, similes, and the substitution of synonyms only until the end of the day's work. Why should you treat the balance of your immortal prose with such contempt?

Every paragraph, every sentence, and even every word should be written with as much care as though you had the last typewriter ribbon on earth. One of the greatest misnomers in the English language is the word rewrite: All you are going to do under the name of rewrite and revise is to polish the existing manuscript. There will come a time when your experience will pay off and every page that comes out of your typewriter will be perfect, but that time has not yet arrived. For the time being, you must give yourself the best possible material.

Your novel will be divided into chapters of a length most convenient to yourself. You know the final length of the finished product. Dividing it into chapters enables you to get a handle on the story. The actual length of your chapters is a decision that you will make for yourself. You broke your outline into chapters for your own convenience, and using a standard length chapter will give you an idea of the progress you are making on the whole thing. Do not finish a chapter at some specific word count, or round it off to the nearest sentence or even paragraph end. The end of the chapter should come at the nearest emotional break. Some of your chapters may run twice the length of the standard you have elected to use, and some may fall very far short of that length. The main thing is that the story maintains its continuity.

Breaking the story into chapters makes it easier for the reader to deal with it. How many times have you become engrossed in a book, and when the time came to set it aside, you looked at your watch and said, "Just one more chapter," and went right on reading. This is the situation that you want to get your reader involved in. Perhaps the easiest type of book to read is the one that presents very short chapters, while the most difficult book I ever tried to read was Judith Rossner's

Looking for Mr. Goodbar. It was not divided into chapters. The body of the narrative had a prologue and an epilogue tagged on, and it was a tribute to my patience and the motivation of being committed to writing a review that I ever finished reading it.

By breaking your novel down into chapters you will be making it much easier for the reader to handle. And you will be making it easier to write, as well.

The three most crucial chapters of your novel are the last three. The second to last carries the final resolution of the problem, the one before that sets the stage with each of the characters in the right place and doing the right thing, while the final paragraph ties up all the loose ends and provides a summation.

Where the first chapter sells the book, the last two chapters sell the next book. You have spent your entire writing time manipulating your characters and with them your reader's vicarious emotions, all with the goal of solving the problem that is gradually worsening chapter by chapter. Now comes the time when your characters must not be allowed to drift off at a tangent: Any potential that you see in any action or dialogue must be ignored or possibly filed away for future use in the next book. Each of your characters has a specific part to play in the unfolding of the plot. What you have thought of in only the most general terms must now be detailed. The atmosphere should be arranged for the greatest support and all the characters lined up to play their parts.

If you have a twist ending in mind, you have probably not thought beyond that final line of dialogue or action. The third from last chapter gives you an opportunity to put the final touches to the problem, the touch that makes the problem even more insoluble than ever (the straw that breaks the camel's back). At the same time you must make sure that all your characters are in the right frame of mind (the villains sneering, the good guys open-mouthed in admiration) and in the right place at the right time. They must be ready to present the facts that you have been saving for the denouement and they must have reasonable access to that information.

If somebody tells what only Great Aunt Agatha could have possibly known, don't suddenly tell the reader that old Great Aunt Aggie whispered this from her deathbed. Have one of the more modern characters be sorting out her books and papers and find this entry in her diary of 1926 or whenever it must have been. Your reader expects to be surprised by the ending but not by the way it is presented.

The final chapter is the summation of the actions of the minor characters. To use the tritest of trite phrases when they "ride off into the setting sun," the last chapter tells what goes on after the sun goes down.

Carmelita readies the cottage for the new tenants, Buck Brenner hands William Spooner his supper in the jail cell. Madeline's dog stands guard over the bitch while she is whelping. Janet's boss at the London *Globe* gives an assignment to a junior reporter, wishes that Janet was back, and goes out to the nearest pub for a quick pint. But don't try to use them all, just one or two as a wind-down. Most mainstream novels start off by devoting one chapter (or maybe a half chapter) to each character to give the reader a thorough understanding of each person, but it is a mistake to try to close a novel with a complete summation of every person who has made an appearance. The final chapter or summation is to be used to tell the reader that now that the problem has been solved, life has gone back to normal.

16.

Reviewing,
Revising,
and Rewriting

Once you have typed "The End" to your creation, take a vacation: go skiing, swimming, surfing, bicycling, play chess, take up needlepoint, or do whatever may take your fancy while the manuscript cools off. Before you start the task of reviewing and revising, you must be able to look upon this child of yours with a certain objectivity. Reading over the day's output a few pages at a time as you type them does not give you the perspective you need to look at the novel as a completed work.

Reviewing and revising is a chore hated with a passion by some writers while others look forward to it as the most important and thus the most rewarding step of producing a novel. I have heard that it was James Michener who said, "I'm not much of a writer, but I'm the best damned rewrite artist in the business." Many writers face the task of reviewing and revising with a willingness, knowing that it is the final polishing stage that makes it fit to be seen in public. Others (myself included) would do almost anything to avoid it. If that seems like an unreasonable attitude, it is colored by the fact that once the complete draft has been finished, the emotional drive has been spent. Revising or rewriting is something like sitting down to a meal ten minutes after you have eaten.

Set your book aside for a period—I would suggest not less than two weeks—so that you can approach it with a fresh look, almost as a stranger would see it. When you have grown tired of your knitting, checkers, or whatever else you have decided upon to occupy yourself, drag your creation out and start reading it again. Even after such a short time you will be amazed at the things you have not seen before. It was on one such occasion that I, who was bragging about my spelling earlier in this book, found that I had written emancipated instead of emaciated.

Sit down and read the book from cover to cover to get the overall picture.

What you are looking for now is any reorganization that is needed in your material. If you copied your detailed outline into two stacks of 3 x 5 cards, this should not be a problem. The continuity of your main plot will be exactly as you have dreamed it up, but you may find parts of the subplot may read better with a little reorganization. Don't do it right now. Make a note of it, and see if there is anything else that you might want to change. Once you have decided on all the structural changes, or alternately decided that the manuscript doesn't need any structural changes, look for areas of expertise that need to be confirmed.

As we did with the romance-suspense novel, where we used information from the encyclopedia and from the tourist bureau in the Bahama Islands, we must admit even if only to ourselves that our sources of information on Nassau leave something to be desired. The next step is to have the book, or at least that passage, read by an expert, in this case somebody who has lived there recently or who has visited there. Most travel agents vacation at these exotic places in order to bring plausibility into their merchandising. Experts in other fields can be used for similar means: firearms experts, antique car buffs, coin collecters, philatelists. Most of these people are only too anxious to help out; it probably has something to do with ego. The thing to do then is to give one of these experts that portion of your book and tell them exactly what you want. If you give them the entire book, there is a good chance that they will see themselves as a self-appointed literary critic, and you don't need any advice on what is wrong with your story line or the characterization (unless this person is somebody whose judgment you trust in the field of genre fiction). I have had much advice leveled at me by people whose only qualification was that they once read a couple of books. I implore you to stay away from these kinds of people. Everybody wants to get his book read and praised, but this is not the time. Wait until you have it finished. Then, if you are really desperate for praise, you can ask your friends to read it.

While you are still considering the overall picture, check the time span. Does the length of time covered seem reasonable? Can what is done be reasonably expected to be accomplished in that space of time or are you developing lifetime friendships in a matter of hours? Have you tried to concentrate a lifetime of experience in a matter of hours? Have you started the book too far in advance of the appearance of the main person? And are you resorting to too many flashbacks to fill in background detail? Do any of your teen-aged characters show the wisdom and experience of maturity? Inversely, do any of your mature characters act like teenagers?

Now what about the point of view? Have you consistently written from the point of view of one person or have you skipped from person to person? And if you have changed the viewpoint, have you made the change obvious? Once you have made the structural changes that are needed and confirmed the consistency of the points of view and timespan, it is time to check the composition, paragraph by paragraph, sentence by sentence, and finally word by word.

A paragraph is not just a bunch of sentences, it is a group of sentences that add a new thought or action to the story. It is at this point that careful insertion of a few good metaphors and similes will lend your work all the sheen of a well-polished gem. The too-frequent use of mediocre metaphors is like calling a spade a bloody shovel.

Above all, don't talk down to your readers. Your reader is there to be entertained, not to have his or her vocabulary tested. Never use a long, nebulous word if you can express a more definite thought in a few short words.

Is your beginning a good hook? Do you draw the reader in? Are your action and character sketches sufficiently provocative to hold the reader's attention and arouse his curiosity?

Do you have sufficient crises and climaxes throughout the story to retain the interest? Have you maintained the pace through the whole story?

Have you made good use of brevity and clarity? Does your reader know everything that needs to be known about the action and characters, and is it written as clearly as possible?

Have you avoided the use of all generalizations? You should throw out any such phrases as "Tony had a peculiar attitude of mind" or "Marcia was wearing a weird dress." The reader is entitled to know why Tony's attitude of mind was peculiar and why Marcia's dress was weird. Don't make up the reader's mind for him; describe the object in question and let the reader make up his own mind as to whether it is peculiar, weird, funny-looking, or even odd-ball.

Have you made use of the reader's senses? Have you appealed to his sight, hearing, smell, and touch when you have described the settings; are you appealing to his general sense of awareness? Are your descriptive passages liberally interspersed with action, or are they like a still photograph in the middle of a movie? Are they long rambling paragraphs that break up the rhythm and the flow of the story?

There is a common fallacy in the minds of many neophyte writers that when a story needs to be cut, it can be done simply by looking at words. You may find that once you have reached the end of your manuscript, it is too long, and I can assure you that looking at words is not the way to cut it. A piece of work cut in this fashion does nothing but dispense with superfluous adjectives and adverbs. You certainly must eliminate these, and one way is to pick a page of your manuscript and count the adjectives. If there are more than two dozen, you are suffering from adjectivitis, a disease for which there is no cure but amputation: the amputation of the pencil.

One of the most frequent faults of the new writer is to over-describe and over-explain. Almost without exception, most lengthy descriptive passages can be dropped without their affecting the complications of the story. Descriptive passages have their use as builders of atmosphere, and as you have seen elsewhere, a good dialogue unstintingly seeded with descriptive phrases may well serve your purpose.

At times the reverse is true. You may get a letter of rejection from an editor hinting that he likes your story, but this particular series of novels runs to a specific number of words, and yours falls about 10,000 words short of that number. For anybody who is mentally prepared to cut the manuscript, this comes as a blow sufficient to send you to the nearest wall to see whether it or your head is the stronger in the ensuing collision. Here, simply do the reverse: Instead of cutting out extraneous descriptive passages and small scenes with your minor characters, put them in. That doesn't mean that you should scatter long descriptive paragraphs throughout the book, but you should put in a few scenes between the minor characters that will have little or no bearing on the outcome of the story's continuity.

In our romance-suspense novel, wherever we find a lag in the transition we could write in a scene with Carmelita and Janet accentuating Carmelita's pidgin English and her street-smart ways, or perhaps Carmelita could have a boyfriend, one of the local gardeners.

A similar thing can be done with our western. You remember that Lou Packett and Madeline Miles were driven out into the countryside, and you could very easily write in a scene where Buck Brenner forms a rescue squad to ride out to find them. Or maybe Madeline's dog, who is enslaved to Lou Packett, wanders off the ranch to find them.

That is not such a bad idea. Earlier I mentioned in chapter eleven that a rapport with animals is a very desirable element, and with such a scene you serve both purposes. It will take a little further rewriting where you develop the friendship between Lou and the dog, but since you are looking for more words, it can do nothing but good.

The place to look for these scenes is in the transitions. If Janet gets in her rented car to drive into town for a lunch date with her bogus cousin and your next scene starts with his greeting her at the hotel, you have a transition that is a natural place for an extra scene. On the way into town she could make a detour and you can write a small scene in there with a false clue (or red herring as the mystery writers like to call them).

If you are trying to cut down your word count, you simply do the reverse. Take out small, unimportant scenes and put two transitions together. This may give you a problem in that you might have to take some important point from that scene and put it somewhere else, but it should not be difficult to do.

Do not be misled by my use of the phrase *word count*. This does not mean that you should increase your word count by 10,000 words by sticking in a couple of 5,000-word descriptive passages telling the reader about the moonlight on the sage in your western, or the sun dropping like a golden orb into the blue waters of the Caribbean in our romance-suspense. Although it is desirable to cut the word count by eliminating extraneous passages, any attempt to increase the word count should be done only with action scenes.

Anything you delete should be lined through with a pencil on the first draft, while any additional material should be typed up on a separate sheet of paper. This should be headed and numbered consecutively (*Insert #1 page 23 where indicated*). Then, on page 23 (or wherever it is to be inserted), write Insert #1 in the margin with an arrow pointing to where you need it to appear. The new material should then be attached to the original page with a paper clip. This method must be used whether you are sending your manuscript out for typing or if you are typing it yourself. Lack of system here will find you sitting at your desk with a disordered pile of paper scattered around you, which is much the way my desk looks at any time between bimonthly clean outs.

17.

The
Final
Marketing

Well, there it is: the end product of your creativity in all its perfection. Not only is it your best possible work; you must make it as attractive as possible. I have never heard of an editor who would buy a manuscript simply because it looked neat, but I have heard of a couple of editors who have rejected manuscripts because of their untidy appearance. The book's final revisions now complete, you should retype or have retyped the entire manuscript. Let's take a look at what you must do to conform with the general standards of presentation.

First off, you must use good quality 8½″ x 11″ white paper. Only type on one side, and leave a 1¼ inch margin all around. This gives the editor room for his comments. I am not being facetious when I say that you should write on only one side of the paper because I have heard of writers using both sides of the paper, presumably because they were not told otherwise. Use pica type rather than the slightly smaller elite type, and double space everything as a courtesy to the editor's eyesight. The title page should carry the title in capitals in the center of the page and just under that your name as you want it to appear on the published version. On the lower left corner, put your true name and address, in care of the agency, if you have an agent. Do not punch any holes in the manuscript or use a binder of any type. Now you take your manuscript to your friendly neighborhood print shop and get half a dozen photocopies made. Be sure that the copies are good and legible. Never should you use carbon copies. Photocopying has made enormous improvements recently and carbon copies are definitely passé and, in addition, more expensive.

Your manuscript is now ready to send off, but you are not ready to send it out yet; there are some things for you to do first. At the beginning of this book you did a survey to help you decide the genre in which you should be writing. Now you must do another survey to decide which publishers you want to see it. *Writer's Market,* an annual publication, lists all of the current publishing houses and the types of books they normally publish, and *Writer's Digest,* a monthly periodical, updates these markets. Most professional assocations, such as the Romance Writers of America, Mystery Writers of America, and National Writers Club, constantly keep this information current with their monthly or bimonthly newsletters. Incidentally, all three of these associations welcome unpublished writers and membership will enable you to keep abreast of current trends. Next, what you need to do is to select perhaps half a dozen of the most likely publishers and write them a query letter.

Not so very long ago you could send your manuscript in to any publisher, and it would sit in what was known as the "slush pile" until somebody got around to reading it and making a decision on it. It was not entirely unknown for a manuscript to disappear for as long as six months at a time in this way, and the publishers became so inundated with these "over the transom" submissions, they simply refused to accept any more. I have heard on very good authority that the chance of a book from the slush pile being published was about five thousand to one, which is why you need to use the query letter or any other means to draw attention to your book.

The query letter should be addressed to an editor at the house you have chosen. You obtain the editor's name from the *Writer's Market* or one of your newsletters. It should be a simple letter; an example follows:

Dear (Editor's name):

I have recently completed a romance-suspense novel, Jewels of the Caribbean. It is about a young Englishwoman journalist who sets out to clear the name of her uncle, an honest man who has been accused of a jewel robbery. Would you be willing to look at a copy? I am enclosing a SASE for your convenience and look forward to hearing from you.

One of two things will happen now. You will either be told that they are not interested in your book for a variety of reasons: They may be overstocked on romance-suspenses; they may only publish men's fiction, or perhaps they are only looking for gothics; or you will be invited to send your manuscript in for a reading. Whatever the answer, you will certainly know a "no" when you see it.

If the answer is yes, then pack a copy of your manuscript with a couple of cardboard stiffeners in a box or a padded envelope with a letter like this:

Dear (Editor's name):

> Thank you for your letter of April 22nd. As you suggested, I am enclosing a copy of my romance-suspense novel, Jewels of the Caribbean. I hope it suits your publishing requirements. Return postage enclosed.

What do you do now? Sit and wait for the replies to come in? Not on your life! You start working on the next book.

You can also submit your manuscript through an agent. This requires a similar technique, so let's take a look at what an agent can do for you. No agent has a magic formula for getting a manuscript published any more than I have a magic formula for writing a successful novel.

A few years ago I went to the largest Writers Conference in the country and I was appalled at what I found. As is usual, the majority of those in attendance were unpublished and quite often unwritten would-be authors. I would expect these people to be full of questions, like what should I write and how should I write it. They were certainly full of questions, but the only questions I heard were, "How do I get an agent", or "Would your agent represent me?" It never seemed to occur to anybody that they should write a book before they started looking for an agent. A few of them had made a start on a book and were horrified at the thought that for nonfiction they might need to write an outline, and a few sample chapters of the complete novel in the case of fiction, before they sold what they had written.

You have a distinct advantage over these people. You have experienced all the frustrations and joys of creating a complete novel, and (if nothing else) you have demonstrated to the world that you have the ability to stay with a project until its conclusion. Through all the years the best way to get an agent has not changed. This is to sell your book to a publishing house and engage an agent to represent you in the contract negotiations, an act the publishers will applaud.

An agent keeps abreast of current happenings in the publishing world and is more likely to match your manuscript with the publisher most likely to need it at that time. Beyond that, the agent's main job is to take care of the dollars and cents side of the business to see that you get the largest possible advance and royalty rates while you take care of the writing. An agent can be used in an advisory capacity when you are uncertain of what to write. This book was written at the suggestion of my agent after he had negotiated a contract, when I had been going along happily writing genre fiction novels.

Writer's Market has a complete list of agents and they should be approached with a query letter in much the same way you approached the publishing houses. If his list of clients is full, an agent may give you an unqualified "no," but then again he might offer to take a look at your book. Unless you have a track record of several published novels, looking at your manuscript is the closest he will come to a "yes." The thing to remember is that no matter how good an agent might be, he cannot sell a poor manuscript. A good manuscript sells itself no matter how good an agent presents it.

There are three types of agents. The first is the most honorable who does not charge a fee to read your work, his lists are always full, and the only way he will represent you is if (1) he has a vacancy on his client list, and (2) if you come highly recommended, or (3) if an editor recommends you. The second agent is no less honorable, and he will charge you a small fee for reading your manuscript with the under-standing that he will give you a thorough critique of it and that if he sells it for you the fee will be reimbursed from his commission. The third agent is less honorable and is usually advertised as a consulting service: He will charge a reading fee and his critique will in fact be a suggestion that he should rewrite it for you at a price.

Of the three types, the second is the most popular. Sure, he charges a fee, but that is only to pay the overhead while your manuscript is keeping him away from his established client's work, which seems to me not an unreasonable attitude to take. Should you sell your manuscript, the first agent may or may not represent you depending on the size of his client list, while the second will almost always take you on, and there will be no further fee for subsequent books. The third agent will charge you a fee for every book you write, although I am not sure how far he will go in suggesting rewrite changes. Anybody I have known who has used this kind of agent has never tried to use them for more than one book.

Once you have shipped your manuscript off to either the publishing house or to your agent, you come to the toughest part: overcoming the depression that falls on you. I said earlier that writing a novel makes every day finish up with a happy ending: Not writing a novel once you have become accustomed to it fills every day with despondency, an emotion that can only be lifted by writing a second novel.

You will be amazed at how much easier it is to write the second one, and you will have learned much from the actual experience of writing the first. You may or may not want to write a similar book, another western or a second romance-suspense. On the other hand, you may find that the problems that you ran into with the first might be more easily dismissed if you change your subgenre. There is nothing to say that you cannot switch from genre to genre. It takes a great many books to stereotype an author and being stereotyped is not the worst thing that can happen to you.

To help you decide what genre your second book will be I have included a list of all the subgenres with the top (sometimes top two) authors in that field. You will note that in an attempt to keep you current, I have only included living authors. With very few exceptions these authors do not restrict themselves to any one subgenre, and there is no reason why you should restrict yourself.

Romance

Historical	Patricia Matthews
Regency	Barbara Cartland, Georgette Heyer
Suspense	Mary Stewart
Contemporary	Janet Dailey
Gothic	Victoria Holt

Action-Adventure

Series	Don Pendleton (The Executioner) Donald Hamilton (Matt Helm)
Espionage	Eric Ambler, John Le Carré
Straight adventure	Graham Greene, Alistair MacLean
Wartime	David Westheimer

Mysteries

Police procedural	Joseph Wambaugh
Private eye	Joe Gores
Innocent bystander	Dick Francis
Locked room and Drawing room	Michael Gilbert
Hard boiled P.I.	Jonathan Latimer
Suspense	Brian Garfield; John D. MacDonald (Travis McGee series)
Western	Louis L'Amour
Occult	Stephen King, Gary Brandner
Science fiction	Isaac Asimov, Jerry Pournelle
Fantasy	J.R.R. Tolkien

It is only my opinion that these are the top authors in these fields. After reading a few books in your alternate genre you may disagree with me, and nothing would give me greater pleasure than to include your name in the above when this book comes out in its next edition.

I hope that this has been of some help to you . Writing is a good hobby and a wonderful form of mental exercise, even if you only do it for your own amusement. It is different from most other hobbies. People who take up writing as a hobby are never satisfied until they see their work in print, unlike the artist who is content to paint a few good pictures without feeling that he should be accorded a gallery showing. Not being satisfied with anything less than the best, you want to see every one of your books in print. Certainly the easiest way to break into print without its costing you a small fortune is in genre fiction. Every genre could certainly use a few more good authors, and I sincerely hope that you turn out to be one of the best. Good luck.

Index